The Life of an Activist

In the Frontlines 24/7

Randy Jurado Ertll

University Press of America,® Inc.
Lanham • Boulder • New York • Toronto • Plymouth, UK

University Press of America,® Inc.
4501 Forbes Boulevard, Suite 200, Lanham, Maryland 20706
UPA Aquisitions Department (301) 459-3366

10 Thornbury Road, Plymouth PL6 7PP, United Kingdom

Library of Congress Control Number: 2013936613
ISBN: 978-0-7618-6135-5 (cloth : alk. paper)—ISBN: 978-0-7618-6136-2 (electronic)

∞™ The paper used in this publication meets the minimum requirements of American National Standard for Information Sciences Permanence of Paper for Printed Library Materials, ANSI/NISO Z39.48-1992.

Cover photograph by Domenico Foschi.

Dedicated to Jesus Christ, a powerful activist
who revolutionized our hearts and minds

Contents

Foreword

Terrence J. Roberts

Randy Jurado Ertll has written about his life as an activist in ways that inspire readers to recalibrate their own lives. His struggles against injustice remind us of the need for continued social action at every level of our existence. Forced from his country of birth as a consequence of unjust regulations, plunged into the chaos of 1970's rural El Salvador, later in that same decade faced with the task of learning to navigate the mean streets of South Central Los Angeles, Randy discovered an incipient desire to change the order of things. He nurtured that kernel even as he expended vast amounts of energy just to outwit the menacing mice, cockroaches, and human vermin that sought to add him to their list of victims. What he saw around him did not mesh with the vision in his own head; Randy saw the reality of poverty and its related ills, but was not inclined to embrace that version of life. No, he could see even then that something better must be in his future.

Indeed, it was "A Better Chance" that awaited him as this organization provided the means for him to attend high school in Minnesota. With that boost, Randy was off and running. And he has not stopped yet! You will read about his foundational experiences in college, his continued growth as a young community organizer, the influential figures in his life, and the fuel that feeds the fire in his belly. His accumulated wisdom over the years is evident as he provides detailed instructions about organization and mobilization for non-profits, and gives fair warning to those who would accept boards of directors and/or bureaucracies at face value. It would be well for budding activists to know that guerilla warfare tactics are not to be disregarded!

Perhaps more than anything else, what Randy gives us is the opportunity to face ourselves in the mirror and ask the hard questions that lurk always at the edge of consciousness. Why am I here on this planet? Is it my job to cry out against the injustice around me? Where is it written on the walls of the universe that someone else, someone besides me, should tackle the issues we all face? What will happen if I don't act? As you read how Randy answers these questions for himself, you may feel an itch to learn more about your role in this human drama or you may find nagging questions insistent upon being answered during all of your waking hours (and maybe disturbing your sleep as well!) Whatever the outcome, remember, your choice is just that, your choice. Neither Randy nor I nor anyone else will say you must be involved.

But, do remember this, the need is great. The time is now.

Terrence J. Roberts, Ph.D., One of the "Little Rock Nine," who desegregated Little Rock Central High School in 1957

Chapter One

Evolution of an Activist

Activists come in all sizes, shapes, colors, and ideologies. But the one thing they have in common is a need to fight for social justice. Activists want to change the world for the better.

I developed a sense of activism and social justice as a small child in El Salvador. I spent my early years in a small village during the 1970s, where plumbing was non-existent and electricity was new. I saw the poverty, the injustices against *campesinos*, and the history of violence. Unfortunately justice and peace never really existed in El Salvador. The Civil War took the humanity away from many people. Children grew up thinking that death was normal; the smell of rotting corpses became an everyday occurrence.

My mother had to sacrifice by coming to work in Los Angeles, California. She left me with my grandparents so that they could raise me in that small village in Usulutan. I lived around nature, with a loving grandmother who lived until 2012. My mother wanted to provide for my grandparents and for me, so she did what thousands of Salvadoran mothers had to do: leave their children behind in order to earn *dolares* in the United States. She eventually did come back to pick me up, and we moved to South Central Los Angeles in the late 1970s.

What a shock that was to a small child. I had to become accustomed to the concrete and violence of urban America. In El Salvador, rural violence was common, but not the same. It definitely was a completely different world when I arrived in the United States. We had to move into apartments where the ceilings were falling, rain leaked inside, plumbing was rusty, and where mice and cockroaches festered, along with thieves, criminals, and murderers who roamed the streets of South Central, looking to buy or sell drugs, steal, or kill.

I attended some of the toughest public schools in California, and began to see how African Americans and Latinos were both fighting for the same scarce resources, and simply trying to survive.

I began to hear about President Jimmy Carter and how he wanted to help the poor. Then Ronald Reagan became President. He pretty much favored the wealthy and had little tolerance for the poor. Many were barely getting by on welfare, food stamps, and minimum wage jobs. Of course, most parents wanted a better future for their children in South Central, but the opportunities were distant and almost unattainable. I had to confront the realities of poverty on a daily basis. This world shaped my own view of working towards social justice.

During high school, I won a scholarship that gave me the chance to spend three years in Rochester, Minnesota as part of the "A Better Chance" (ABC) program. I had to take a standardized test, fill out applications, and went through a formal interview to get accepted. Through this program, I was finally able to compare the discrepancies among three worlds: El Salvador, Los Angeles, and the Midwestern United States. Attending high school in Minnesota opened windows of my mind and provided experiences that were incredible. When I first enrolled at John Marshall High School in tenth grade, I met middle-class whites, poor whites who were kind, and wealthy whites who cared and wanted to help minority kids to succeed.

Slowly but surely I began to read more books in high school and I successfully graduated in 1991. I wanted to attend college and decided to apply to Occidental College to come back to my family. I had always felt some sort of guilt that I was given a ticket out of the ghetto and had left my mother and two sisters behind.

Now that I think about it, I had been an activist for my family ever since I was in elementary school. I was the small, English-speaking adult who negotiated paying the bills over the phone, or went to Pacific Bell with my mother. I was able to tell the landlords when the toilet was clogged or when the roof was leaking, or about to fall again. I had to call the Housing Rights organizations so they could take legal action against owners to fix the rundown houses or apartments that we rented. I did not see it happening, but I was becoming an advocate for my family. I grew up spending my vacation days with my mother, while she worked in the sweatshops of Downtown Los Angeles. I also remember babysitting my youngest sister and always worrying about her safety. By the time I got to high school, I was a bit like "Little Man Tate," but with an inclination toward the arts and literature.

During summer breaks in high school, I tried to get my African American and Latino neighbors to develop a violence and crime-prevention group. Looking back I also wanted to help develop a truce between the 18th Street and the Rolling 40 Crips gangs. Many of the mothers of the drug dealers came to the first meeting to see how we could help reduce violence. A few days later some suspicious individuals decided to loosen the bolts on the wheels of our Camaro, sending a clear message that they were not too happy and that police were not welcome in that neighborhood. I was somewhat naïve and idealistic. I believed in the goodness of humanity.

Later on, I began to "wake up" politically in college. I began to read and question things. I was enthralled by learning more about politics and how power works. I began to want to change the world.

In the following chapters I want to share all of you what it takes to become an activist, and how to survive as an activist over the long haul. My perspective may seem harsh at times, but I want to paint a realistic picture of the pros and cons of being an activist. It is no piece of cake. Being a community organizer is one of the toughest jobs in the world. If you want to change the world, you must first learn about yourself, accept your strengths and weaknesses, and strive to mature.

Activism is not for the meek or timid. It is like stepping into a Mixed Martial Arts competition. You may have to train for years or decades — and there is no guarantee that you will win. You have to learn every kick, punch, arm / leg locks, and takedowns. You must work on endurance, perseverance, and resilience. Those same attributes apply to being an activist. You may begin the journey angry, very angry like I was. But gradually you see that you need to pace yourself to make social activism a way of life. You have to learn to love yourself — and love others too.

You have to train your body, mind, soul, and spirit when you decide to become an activist for the long haul. You always have the right to quit or change career paths. But an activist has to be committed and ready to face the heat. At times it will be exhilarating, especially when you win your first battles or successfully organize a campaign. You will learn from defeats and triumphs. Your heart will pound, you will get hungry, your hands, feet, and forehead will sweat when you choose to confront the status quo and bureaucracies that refuse to change.

This book will offer an opportunity to take a sneak peek in the life of an activist. I will briefly discuss social justice giants like Martin Luther King Jr., Malcolm X, and Cesar Chavez. They chose to become activists in different stages of their lives and each one was thoroughly unique and courageous. Many people despised them while they were alive. We now have somewhat sanctified them, but each had to sacrifice and suffer very much during their lives. They even sacrificed the safety and comfort of their own families in voluntarily choosing to defend the rights of others. They were not stingy, self-centered, or selfish. They chose to give their lives for the greater good of society, wanting to change society for the better. They did not tolerate or sit idle and watch injustices. They chose to stand up and advocate for others. Hopefully this book will inspire you to further analyze some social movements and individual activists. If you choose the path of becoming an activist, congratulations. You are more than welcome into the club.

It is life-changing to take a stand on an issue, defend the rights of others, or provide a voice for those who have no voice. To provide strength for others. To provide a vision and a mission. To provide goals that can be attained. To provide leadership and love to humanity. In the process, you will begin to understand yourself better, and you may even find spirituality.

There are some activists who get lost along the way. They become skeptical, bitter, frustrated, and pissed-off at the world. But the purpose of this book is to take a realistic view, and to see the bad, but show more of the good. We know that our society is full of corruption, envy, selfishness, and greed. You have to avoid becoming fatigued and seeing only the negative in life. You have to create optimism from your soul, and then others will begin to follow you and trust you.

One of the purposes of this book is to inspire activists to work for a more just and equitable society, to create better opportunities for others, and create a sense of optimism. When individuals believe in themselves, they can help to change the world, baby. Yes, change the world.

Y porque no?

Chapter Two

Angry and Bitter
Is Not Necessarily the Answer

To resist bitterness, activists must reach for our better angels and inner inspiration. Stay focused on the injustice itself and to decide to do something about it, rather than sitting idle or lamenting the inequities. As a young, angry, and sometimes judgmental activist, I refused to "drink the Kool-Aid" and just pretend that everything was fine and dandy. I knew that certain things in our society needed to be improved urgently and dramatically.

Former Secretary of Labor Robert Reich stated in an interview with *The Progressive* magazine in the October 2012 edition, "Nothing good happens in Washington D.C., or for that matter, in state capitals, unless good people outside Washington or those state capitals make it happen. Unless they push very hard. Unless they're organized, mobilized, and energized to force the political system to respond. The rest of us have to do more than simply vote, pay our taxes, and respond to summonses to be juries. Citizenship goes far beyond those three. We've got to insist on being heard." (Cook, 2012, p. 36)

One day at a time. One step at a time. Becoming an activist can become hell on earth. Working for non-profit money is always tight and demands are never-ending. It can make you question why you would choose what seems at times like a thankless path. But I came to realize that I work for non-profits and write advocacy columns because I want to speak for others, who did not get a ticket out of an oppressive situation. I wanted to share untold stories.

Becoming an activist can be an escape from an abusive household. As a young child, you are practically stuck with your family. Often a social worker never arrives to save you from abuse and neglect, and take you to a loving foster home. To be fair, county employees often say that they are overwhelmed and cannot do more, especially when some family members know

5

how to take advantage of the system and hide abuse from social workers and law enforcement.

At the same time, not every activist comes from underprivileged circumstances. Those who didn't suffer abuse from families, police, school districts, or other institutions may simply have a burning desire to give back and make our society more equitable. They may empathize with the needy, and use their education, economic privilege, and knowledge for social justice.

Regardless of their background, those who are sensitive to injustice will want to change the world, but the world often does not want to play along. Many believe that marching, picketing, shouting, posting messages on Facebook, writing on walls, getting arrested, having all night discussions, will lead to social change. Well, maybe. Corruption and money interests are so entrenched that many activists begin as idealists and dreamers in high school or college, but once they graduate they must pay their student loans and get any job that is available. Some forget their activist roots and choose to become part of the status quo and mainstream. Of course, you can definitely make positive changes by also going to work for corporations and running for elected office. George McGovern and Sargent Shriver are great examples of the eternal optimistic activists who want to change the world — and in some ways they did. McGovern passed away in 2012 and one time I had the honor to hear him speak in person in Pasadena. Of course, I was not fully familiar with his own life story and struggles. Former President Richard Milhous Nixon hated George McGovern and any progressive activists. The L.A. Times reported:

> Four years later, with antiwar sentiment at a pitch, he ran for president again. Almost immediately, McGovern became a target of attacks that grew into Watergate. President Nixon's aides saved their worst for other Democrats, because Nixon thought McGovern would be easier to beat. Nonetheless, they took steps to insert a Nixon 'plant' into McGovern's campaign. In his authoritative 1976 book, 'Nightmare: The Underside of the Nixon Years,' J. Anthony Lukas documented how Nixon's aides did better than a single 'plant.' They placed a spy among reporters covering McGovern's campaign, they sent a private investigator to infiltrate his state campaign in California, and they inserted still another spy into his national headquarters near Capitol Hill. This spy provided a floor plan, including electrical outlets and air ducts. Nixon's men used it in several attempts to install electronic listening devices inside McGovern headquarters. Only after failing at this did they break into and bug the Democratic National Committee at the Watergate complex (Meyer, 2012, p. 1)

McGovern lost his bid for the Presidency against Richard Nixon but he became a national hero for progressives and activists throughout the United States. He suffered much and he had tragic experiences in life. His daughter Teresa, who suffered from depression and alcoholism, was found in December 1994 in Madison, Wis., frozen to death in the snow after an evening of drinking. She was 45 and the mother of two. In her diary, McGovern read how she had suffered as a youngster through his long campaigns and his endless nights in the Senate and how she had missed him and felt desolate, rejected and abandoned. McGovern was overwhelmed with guilt. 'I'd give everything I have, and I mean everything' he told The Times, 'for one more afternoon with [her], just to tell her how much I loved her' (Meyer, 2012, p. 1). The price many activists have to pay is tremendous.

As one of those who has intentionally stuck with this path of madness, here's why I did: Growing up in the ghetto, not many opportunities existed. One can gang bang, sell drugs, see the ravages of domestic violence, and witness and learn from parents the bad words and the beating down of children with fists, belts, hangers, wire cords, a hug and a *lo siento*. Children go to school hungry, with old clothes, scratches on their face, welts on their back, and trampled self-esteem.

Kids often aspire to be superheroes or villains. Some become superheroes by choosing activism. Others became villains, by beating and killing those in their own community. The abusive households can take away the sense of humanity, and stabbing or shooting someone is a method of releasing that fury. Law enforcement agencies seem to know only how to place troubled youth in juvenile halls, and Latino and Black youth in prison. They see these youth as a threat to society. The conservative attitude is "If you do the crime, you do the time."

The young activist wants to change those injustices through protests and writing. The old methods of fasting and sit-ins are still effective, but no longer that trendy. Also, hard-core activists, like Cesar Chavez and Gandhi, did heroic fasts for twenty or thirty days. Once, Cesar Chavez fasted and sacrificed for so long — 36 days — that he injured some of his internal organs. Imagine that.

Activists who come here from other countries will say we were hardcore — we were willing to give our lives for the revolution back home, but had to come to the U.S. to avoid being murdered. Many of these *activistas* — also called *comunistas* — became capitalistas with a lower case "c" once they were accustomed to the U.S. capitalist way of life. Many worked hard, bought cars, and a home, a nice pool, and saved some extra *dolares*. They sent wonderful pictures to their home countries, showing off their wealth while the *compatriotas* were still starving and fighting there. Being an activist in the United States is very different to being an activist in countries that are known to *physically eliminate* those troublemaker activists.

But those activists who do get full-time jobs at non-profits in the United States often find they are paid crumbs, barely able to pay the bills, rent, and buy food. Unless you get lucky and end up with a well-established non-profit that pays very well.

In the 1980s, among the Central American solidarity activists, you could tell who were the true believers — the ones that had the old beat-up car, rented a room, and remained activists — creating homemade cardboard signs, going to *marches*, going to late night debriefing and planning meetings at Denny's, McDonalds, or IHOP. Many activists had to do their organizing in secret, since in the 1980's Ronald Reagan would order the FBI to investigate and infiltrate "agitators."

Meanwhile, intellectual activists were getting their Bachelor of Arts, Masters, or PhD's at prestigious universities. These were the street-smart and book-smart intellectual activists, the ones able to read about Karl Marx, Mao, Che Guevara, Malcolm X, Cesar Chavez. The ones who were lucky enough to make it out of the barrio, and into a college or a university. The ones who would one day come back to the 'hood and "save the masses" through their wealth of knowledge and legal expertise.

But we waited and they never came. Many became councilmembers, school board members, and state elected officials, and Congressional members. But they remained invisible or ineffective in helping to resolve the issues of poverty and violence.

We waited and waited in South Central. No one came. We were beaten, robbed, and murdered and we waited for that activist to come and save us. But no one came. By then they were too busy studying and going corporate. After all, no one said life is fair. Especially in the ghetto — where only a few make it out. Most kids have only the gang-bangers and police officers as role models. Many youth begin to sag their pants like the gang bangers, or fantasize about being a police officer in order to get to carry and shoot a gun.

The few who do get out choose different career paths, and very few decide to become lifelong activists, since there ain't no real money in advocating for social justice. It's about sacrifice and fighting for others, even when they may not be aware that an activist is giving his or her life for "la causa," the cause.

Even dating back to the '70's, only a few believed in fighting for *la causa* to the extent that Cesar Chavez and Dolores Huerta (co-founder of the United Farm Workers — UFW) fought for it. Activists need not compare themselves to Cesar Chavez, Marian Wright Edelman, Martin Luther King, Jr., Nelson Mandela, Gandhi, or Malcolm X. But one must be original. Yes, you can learn from these great leaders, who also had many weaknesses and flaws. But they stood out. They chose to give their lives to help others. You cannot replicate them since they are unique. We can admire and emulate some of their ideology and principles. But would you be willing to give up your entire life for a social cause? We may choose to hope to live up to the commitment of Dolores Huerta, Marian Wright Edelman, Monica C. Lozano, Maria Elena Durazo, Connie Rice, and many other unsung heroes that also merit attention and credit. Many are unknown and continue to work in their own communities to make a difference — on a daily basis. Many do not seek nor want attention, which is admirable. Some are quiet corporate activists — who hold positions of great influence and power, and quietly donate to worthy social causes.

Some hard core, grassroots activists inevitably begin to attract unrequested attention by the media and begin to accumulate detractors and critics. This is exactly what happened to Malcolm X and even to Jaime Escalante, the former popular teacher from Garfield High School. Their colleagues began to resent their popularity and fame.

Activists must ask themselves: Am I willing to give my life for this issue or social cause, or will I choose to run for elected office to try to make changes within the system? George Orwell wrote the powerful and legendary book *Animal Farm* that I had not read until recently. Russell Baker wrote the preface for the book, where he states "There is an aloneness about Orwell, an insistence on being his own man, on not playing along with the team as the loyal politician is so often expected to do, or else. This independence is brilliantly illustrated in his classic essay 'Politics and the English Language,' showing how politicians twist the language to distort and deceive. The essay amounts to an act of treason within the political trade. The man is trying to make it harder for a politician to fool enough of the people enough of the time to gain power" (Orwell, 2003, xviii).

In searching for answers, let me retrace my steps as a student activist, and present my own struggle to get a job where one could make social changes.

Back in the day, I made a deal with God in front of the Occidental College library. I spoke to God as I usually would do, in times of a crisis. I said, "If I graduate, I will use my knowledge to try to help others." I knew there were times when I could not help even myself — but hey, I was nineteen years old. Nothing was gonna stop me, the world was mine. (That was before I really started losing my hair!)

Damn, those classes at "Oxy" — Occidental College — were tougher than going to boot camp, or juvenile hall. The professors had heavy credentials and demanded much from each of us as students. No cutting corners or cheating was allowed. Also, no memorization either, since a liberal arts education is designed to prepare you to analyze, think, critique, see different sides of an issue, and not be dogmatic or close-minded. Hell, that is what knowledge is supposed to be about — learning and sharing, disagreeing in a civil and respectful manner. Agreeing to disagree. Understanding that each individual has a different life experience and point of view. True learning takes us out of our comfort zone.

I have to admit that I would fall asleep in certain classes, not that they were necessarily boring. I was exhausted from my night job. Yes, it's embarrassing, but I would fall asleep in Professor's Boesche's philosophy class. I missed so much knowledge when my neck was too weak to keep me awake.

The cap I wore did not help either — it covered my closed eyes. I am proud that at I least tried, by attending class and passing. Rousseau, Locke, and Hobbes would say "good enough." Like Jack Tripper (Johh Ritter) would say in Three's Company 'I'm so ashamed.'

Also, I was too busy partying with my homeboys from the 'hood, and getting lost. But I started to read those radical books by Oscar Zeta Acosta, the biography of Malcolm X, the history of Latin America, Parenti's books on education and those crazy, radical books by Saul Alinsky on how to organize and mobilize. Of course, some may say that the teachings of Alinsky are a bit boring. However, the windows of my mind were opening and my soul was becoming restless. Is this what a rookie activist feels? Maybe.

I started to think, hell, if Chicanos protested in East L.A., if Blacks marched, got arrested, and murdered in the '50's and '60's while fighting for civil rights, if Central Americans were tortured and murdered in their countries, and if Mexicans protested in the "La Noche de Tlatelolco," then why are Blacks and Latinos not outraged and protesting in South Central Los Angeles? Well, Blacks did protest during the Watts riots in the 1960's. But so many other groups did not.

While I was thinking these things, it was one year before the 1992 L.A. Riots. Before the new era of Civil Disobedience, and the uprising of the poor against police brutality and careless politicians. You know the type of politicians to which I am referring, the ones who are your best friends when they run for office, but once elected they forget about you and don't want you to call them by their first name, instead requesting to be addressed as *honorable.* They no longer look, act, or dress the same. Some of their field representatives begin to emulate this attitude, and many become arrogant. Of course, many other elected officials do not forget who their friends are, and do not deny their roots or past. I could list many names of elected officials/politicians who are, in fact, doing great work.

Man, I had to grow up and wake up fast in April 1992. Reading books was not enough. I did an internship with a councilman who fought for the poor, but who at that time had a drug problem. I did an internship at CARE-CEN to fight for the human rights of Central American refugees, and continued working all-nighters doing security at L.A. Swim Stadium and falling asleep in some of my Oxy classes. I worked to buy my books and to help pay my mom's rent. I worked during the day as a Recreational Assistant for the City of Los Angeles. I engaged in menial work — real hard work, in areas where your life was also at risk. I had no time to waste. I had to continue reading, writing, passing my classes. I also began to attend those good old radical meetings to plan protests, marches, and press conferences. I was hooked. Thus I became a junkie — of activism.

Nothing would stop me. We began the Central American Student Association (CASA), and the L.A. Times did a cover magazine story about us. I wasn't featured in the story, perhaps because I did not look ethnic enough. But hell, I had been too busy getting jumped, to understand the significance of my light skin. It kept me from being fully accepted in the ghetto. Hey, thugs have to unleash their hatred and rage on somebody right? Whether it is that ghost-looking, "skeleton kid" or a recent *mojado* from Oaxaca. Or, as we were called at Foshay Middle School (now called Foshay Learning Center), "fucking beaners." Chicanos would call us *ceretos*. It is not a very nice word. Some murders took place due to the use of certain bad words. And you don't want to know the kinds of names some kids are called at home. No wonder our self-esteem was not up to par.

The power of words can build someone up, or beat them down. We were beaten down through words, by gangs and rogue police officers. But sometimes we replicated the violence and repeated the same bad words. We were being socialized to hate, and to perpetuate the violence.

I began to figure this out during my years at Oxy, but meanwhile my community was still being beat down in the ghetto. No opportunities, no escape. Only domestic violence victims know this pain. Children and adults who were beaten, raped, and called horrendous names understood that county social workers and therapists would not save them, that police usually arrived late, when the beating was long since over. Police officers would say, "It is a family issue or a civil matter." Maybe in a few cases they took action and saved the children from hell. That was rare.

Sometimes the damage is so deep it takes decades to recuperate, or perhaps one never fully recuperates. Let's not forget Rodney King. Millions of dollars could not save him from the addictions and the memories of abuse. He grew up as a good kid in Altadena, was a good Jehovah's Witness, but he had addictions and demons that would not leave him alone.

Like they say, "you can take the kid out of the hood, but you cannot take the hood out of the kid." That "hood" is still there, the beer, alcohol, drugs. Rodney King moved to Rialto, trying to rebuild his life, but the drugs caught up with him. What a way to numb the pain. That fuckin' pain doesn't go away, even with crack or methamphetamines. The shit that will make you sell your soul to the devil, will force you to sell your body. That shit will make you sell your own children to the devil.

Even the churches can't help you. Pastors, priests, and rabbis cannot pray it away. Your family cannot help you, because they are broke and damaged too. Fucking drugs.

The activist is expected to change all those realities, and to continue fighting for social justice, sometimes in the middle of bullets, drugs, police busts, and gang warfare. The activist has to be willing to take the hits. Politicians love activists who do not target or criticize them. They are the "house activists, the ones that play the game to get a pay check. The ones that will betray the community when they see that cash flashing. Similar to the former felon or drug addict with two strikes, who has to become an informant to the police. He or she has no choice, and thus will infiltrate and rat on any community group or effort. Even a few of Malcolm X's bodyguards betrayed him. Malcolm X was hated by many envious and jealous people while he was alive. He was a charismatic, inspirational, a great orator, and an effective organizer. But just like other activists after death he became a folk hero. He even got his face on a U.S. postal stamp. Ain't that some shit! No one wants to be your friend while alive, but then all of a sudden, T-shirts with your images are selling like hot cakes. Everyone gets good jobs by saying they were your homeboy or homegirl. Yet when you were marching, protesting, getting arrested, no one knew you.

Who wants to be friends with a broke-ass activist anyway? You have to be Bill Gates to buy friends and to get buildings named after you. Or a crooked politician who knows how to distribute favors and funds in order to get future consultant contracts. Jack Abramoff admitted that he was able to buy at least one hundred members of Congress with gifts and by securing jobs for their chiefs of staff in prestigious lobbying, advocacy, and public relations firms.

The following were my baby steps, while attending Occidental College, in learning to be an activist: attending a union protest in downtown Los Angeles through MEChA (Movimiento Estudiantil Chicano de Aztlan), going to a weekend training program through the unions, then realizing that I do not like shouting or screaming during rallies, which meant that perhaps unions were not a good fit. I met with an ACORN recruiter, who wanted to pay me $6,000 per year. My mom made more in the downtown L.A. sweatshops. I immediately said, "hell no." The ACORN representative became upset at my rebelliousness. An activist has to learn not to go with the flow or become a "yes" person. You have to learn to question things, especially contracts that include small print.

I also began to attend the Movimiento Estudiantil Chicano de Aztlan/ Association of Latin American Students (MEChA/ALAS) meetings at Oxy. No, they were not Communists or Socialists. Flashback: I remember that I invited an Anglo student from Texas who was a conservative Republican. One of the Oxy Mexican American students said out loud "What the fuck is that white boy doing here?" I was so embarrassed since I had naively invited him to our meeting. That kind of closed mindedness made me start to think and realize that maybe *centroamericanos* were not that welcomed, either.

After we created the Central American Student Association (CASA) — I began to attend those meetings. But they were more interested in ethnic cooking and other cultural activities, while I wanted to march or protest. I had new tennis shoes and I wanted to walk! Not just talk but walk, too. I wanted to be active — to make a statement. So many dreams, so much energy, enthusiasm, and idealism to share with the world. I was so young.

1992: The L.A. Riots gave me an advanced degree in social injustices. The truth of the matter is that if the beating of Rodney King had not been captured on video, the same brutality and insanity would probably still be a normal occurrence in L.A.'s poor areas, even today. I saw brutality and violence on a daily basis. I lived it in the 1980's and early 1990's. During these two decades countless individuals were beaten by rogue Los Angeles police officers, who were influenced by then Chief Daryl Gates. Gates liked to portray himself as a tough-as-nails, no-holds-barred cop. He was willing to use force by any means necessary against the so-called bad guys.

During that time, the Los Angeles Police Department's (LAPD's) mission became murky and blurry. Some LAPD officers who were fighting against the thugs became thugs themselves, engaging in unethical and illegal activities under the protection of their badge. Many felt unrestrained power with the badge, baton and gun. Many officers were seen as an occupying force that did not live in the areas where they patrolled. Racism was not subliminal but obvious.

Then the officers who had savagely beat Rodney King during a traffic stop the year before were acquitted. People in South Central and Central L.A. were outraged. They were all too familiar with such inequities and injustices. The rage exploded in one of the most destructive riots in U.S. history. I remember how angry I was. I saw the looting, the immigrants getting beaten, the fires, the chaos. The insanity and injustices of it all.

A few of the positive outcomes of the riots were that the LAPD was forced to reform, Gates resigned as chief, and the Christopher Commission was created. The Christopher Commission came up with many proposals for reform, including revising the City Charter to make the chief of police subject to term limits. Also, a few young activists emerged and were transformed into community leaders.

But it is also important to point out that the media chose to portray the L.A. riots as a white, black, and Korean issue.

The Latino community was mostly ignored in the coverage. The main Latino spokesperson to emerge was actor Edward James Olmos, who on live television decided to take a broom and asked others to join him in cleaning up Los Angeles, after the looting and out-of-control fires initiated by arsonists.

Despite Latinos' invisibility to the media, the riots served as a wake-up call to the broader Latino community. It ignited concern largely from Central American immigrants who had quietly endured mistreatment by police for years. Street vendors, day laborers, and youths began gathering at community meetings, telling their stories of harassment and abuse.

Fear of the LAPD was particularly pronounced among school-age teens, who were frequently profiled as gang members — many still are — just for walking home from school with their friends. The fallout of the verdict meant elected officials would now have to begin hearing concerns raised in Latino neighborhoods about police misconduct. It spread not only to questions about the LAPD, but to criticism of how the Los Angeles County Sheriff's Department treated Latinos as well.

Also, the real underlying political and socioeconomic issues were finally addressed by political and business leaders. Activists such as Dr. Maulana Karenga had been denouncing injustices for many years, and had risked his life by being a warrior in the frontlines of South L.A.

Two decades later, we have a chief of police who believes in community policing, and a City Council that actually acknowledges certain social justice issues. However, we still have a long way to go and the injustices of the past still linger.

Areas such as South L.A., Koreatown, Pico-Union/Westlake, and other high poverty communities continue to be neglected. Liquor stores, cheap motels, and prostitution are still commonplace in South L.A. and other poor areas. The business leaders of Los Angeles have not done enough to bridge the gap between rich and poor.

The real question going forward should be, how will future elected officials help to create real jobs and opportunities in poor, neglected areas that have not improved much since 1992? We need to hold political candidates' feet to the fire when they promise to help revitalize South L.A. and other poor neglected areas.

The continual challenge is to educate youth and train them to be leaders. Otherwise, the same vicious cycle of poverty will continue and the city's poor areas will remain neglected, dangerous and with no real hope. Let's just pray that real change will one day arrive. Let's not wait another 20 years.

I thought I could rest a little bit when the reforms were put in place after the riots. But no, then Governor Pete Wilson endorsed Proposition 187. He wanted to take away the rights of immigrants to obtain medical care and other civil rights. Proposition 187 was a wedge issue that Gov. Wilson chose to champion, so he could get reelected by demonizing immigrants. I hit the streets, volunteering through Coalition L.A. by walking precincts with Don Smith, a well-known religious leader who happens to be an Oxy alumnus. We walked and distributed material against Proposition 187. We found many acculturated and assimilated Latinos who supported Proposition 187 and were blatantly opposed to any immigrant rights. They had already forgotten where they came from. Sad, but true. Similar to the way in which two Latino Oxy students (who ran track & field) would question whether a friend and I belonged at the Oxy gym. They had developed an attitude of superiority and acted as if they wanted to keep their own people in check. Then, to add insult to injury, an African-American Clancy's cafeteria worker at Oxy asked my roommate, Donald from New Mexico, whether we were Oxy students or not. She asked us for student identification and even took us into her office to make sure the IDs were legitimate. She stated, "That is not you in the picture," when in fact it was. She just could not understand why the name on my i.d. was of European extraction. Talk about getting profiled by your allies. Then there was the white Oxy coach who slammed the door in front of me, since he did not want me to work out in the gym. When I went to see the head coach he just said, "You have to be tolerant."

Yeah right, not when getting profiled and mistreated at my own campus, while was paying tuition, and room and board. Not cheap at all. This type of jerk behavior should not be tolerated, since many times discrimination and racism is subliminal. I am simply sharing some life experiences. Some may say, "you are too sensitive. "Well, not when my own community has been mistreated by colonizers and oppressors for centuries. But a mature activist must not hold grudges or take revenge.

I graduated from Occidental College in 1995, wanting to change the unfair economic system in El Salvador. I returned to El Salvador, full of dreams, illusions, and fantasies. Little by little those illusions burned out. I began to see that the former combatants from both sides were forgotten. The leaders kept the power and money. So what the hell is new? The oppressed eventually become the oppressors. Money and power had become the magic formula.

Even though I was disillusioned with politics in El Salvador, when I returned to the U.S. I still believed in the political process. I was enamored with helping candidates. I thought that voter registration, forums, phone banking, and mailings would make a difference. Hell yeah, for the few who got elected, and who did not forget who sweated for them while precinct walking. Many politicians soon forget who helped them. Another requirement of the activist trade is to always be preoccupied. It seems that it is a personality trait to always be planning to organize or to tackle another issue.

My calendar was already filled up — even in college. No time to waste. I was constantly thinking of how to make social change and who to defend next. Facebook did not exist during those days. Those were the good old days when social networking did not suck up so much of our time, and when the government could not trace our every spoken and written word. E-mail was it. Boy, could we create some awesome e-mail group lists to motivate and mobilize hundreds of people.

Now with Facebook, you are lucky if you can mobilize people for a social justice cause. Many do not really pay attention to the posts or invitations to political rallies or meetings. However, these social network tools can help to spread the message about how our wealth disparities continue to grow. I do have to give credit to Professor Caldwell from the Occidental Diplomacy and World Affairs class, where I learned about globalism and other key issues. We were taught to think further and to question political decisions. We learned about the Cold War, the repressive measures used by certain governments, U.S. interests in foreign countries, and we learned to analyze various diplomatic political theories.

I have to take this opportunity to also thank English Professors Deborah Martinson and Professor Thomas Burkdall. I still remember when Professor Martinson finally wrote on my essay: "You are a good writer." And I began to believe that I was. Deep in my heart I always knew that I wanted to be a good writer, I just needed the confidence. Boy, oh boy, do teachers and professors have a major impact in our lives. They can build us up through their comments or break us down.

Let me share a story with you. I was recommended to be a student in an MBA non-profit management degree program at a local university. I thought, what a wonderful opportunity. Then, I had a professor who wrote on one of my papers something denigrating and insulting. That same day I decided to withdraw from that university and I pursued my education elsewhere. The Dean had recommended for me to take four courses while employed fulltime. Terrible advice. I am glad that only ended up paying them $5,000 for a few weeks of enrollment and not the over $100,000 that the whole program cost. It is important for minority students to be aware of colleges and universities who simply want their money, via Federal student loans that are easy to obtain through the Free Application for Federal Student Aid (FAFSA). Sometimes students complete their degrees, but cannot obtain any decent jobs since no one recognizes the names of some of these colleges/universities that set up shop at various locations or via on-line courses.

Fortunately, I applied and decided to obtain my Masters in Organizational and Leadership Studies (MLOS) from Azusa Pacific University (APU). What a wonderful experience. I obtained my Master's degree. Talk about being respected and uplifted by professors who wrote professional comments and feedback on my written papers. I did learn quite a bit at Azusa Pacific University, and I recommend it to other young minorities. They are on the conservative side, but it is important for progressives and conservatives to learn from one another. The professors and students did not make fun of other people's ethnic heritage. Thank goodness.

The key is to respect other people's thoughts and opinions and to not judge people on their skin color, or even if they are bald or shave their head. Not everyone who shaves their head is a gang member, skinhead, or ex-convict. Many athletes and professionals now choose to shave their head and they should not be profiled. The main negative incident that I had at Azusa Pacific University (APU) was when an Azusa Police Department patrol car decided to shine the bright patrol light on me when I was talking to a class-mate in the parking lot. There was no legitimate reason for them to do that, and it is an example of how certain law enforcement individuals do in fact profile based on physical looks or the type of car one drives.

What APU really needs is a better security system to protect the safety of their students and surrounding community members, and to establish a good relationship with community groups and activists within Azusa. Colleges and universities need to invest in and be more involved with the surrounding communities. Occidental College, USC, and UCLA have developed model programs of how students give back to the community through tutoring or mentoring programs. But more can be done and achieved. To help more inner city students to succeed.

On another note, it is important to point out that debates can sometimes be never-ending among activists and you need to be careful not to get caught up by infighting. That will destroy any social movement. The Occupy Movement could have been more effective if individual leaders would have emerged to continue tackling specific issues for the long term. However, they chose to not have specific leaders, and the enthusiasm fizzled. Law enforcement also did a good job of infiltrating and creating chaos among the Occupy Movement. Also, they mistakenly chose to take over certain public spaces, creating an opportunity for city governments and law enforcements to pass punitive restrictions of gatherings in public spaces such as parks or around city halls. The debates and discussions were endless.

Therefore, learn but be wary of the philosophical activists, the ones that just love to question everything and just like to discuss issues in a never-ending manner. They will sap your energy, and most likely shoot down your ideas. They sometimes feel and act as if they know everything there is to know about activism and social movements, since maybe they picketed or marched once or twice. Others expect to get paid just for simply claiming to be a hard core activist who knows what's up or knows some homies.

Sometimes, some community members may ask: "who is more hard-core, the environmental activist or the immigrant rights activist?" Activists have a variety of philosophies, personalities, and backgrounds. Overall, we have to respect the housing rights activists, health disparities activists, police brutality activists, Occupy Movement activists and many others career activists. Many make sacrifices to be successful and they give up time with their families so they can attend many meetings, community events, and mobilizations.

One pressing problem is that many careers in activism do not offer reliable retirement plans. What does an activist do with just a tiny social security check? Live in a car, truck, trailer, or with friends, or unwelcoming family members. Some family members will say, "Well, since you went to college, why the hell are you moving in with your mom or dad, now that you are 30 or 40 years old?" I am telling you, it is not easy being an activist. The expectations and demands are endless. If you get an education and you come from a poor background, then your family may rely on you to save them, too. To pay their bills. To solve their issues. What a burden to carry — for decades and decades. Sometimes some family members may begin to see you as a walking ATM machine. However, if you become successful enough and earn a good salary, it is fulfilling to help others when we are able to do so. Sometimes helping others does not have to be monetarily but through kind and uplifting words.

To make matters worse, we are expected to not even have a right to enjoy life or own a home. An activist is expected to be there for everyone else, except for himself or herself. You have to drain your blood and donate it and not even expect to get paid, while others seek to take credit for your sacrifices. Once you turn 40, the new young activists who are 20 will not recognize your work or efforts. They will say: "We are the real dreamers and the real activists since we camped out with the Occupiers and led marches. Where were the old men and women from the 1980s?" The Millennials may feel that the Generation X did not do enough to change society.

Eventually most activists end up getting married, having children, and perhaps caring for an ailing mother or father. Then they no longer have much free time for protesting, and they become invisible or forgotten.

Social justice activists choose the crazy life. A life of endless meetings, events, networking, and raising money. The life of not eating well, since you are too busy planning change. Starbucks coffee becomes one of your best allies to keep you going. Once you learn the grassroots ropes and have an education to back up your credentials, you can begin to apply to be an Executive Director. Yes, Executive Director. No more organizer, but an administrator who has evolved to manage staff, create and balance a budget, develop and implement programs, write grants to foundations, develop partnerships and collaboratives, organize an annual fundraiser, and establish good communication and trust with the board of directors and community members. The administrators/management must also establish relations with cities, school districts, elected officials, police departments, fire departments, and deal with the jealousy and envy of other activists or executive directors who are struggling to maintain their jobs and survive. At any given time they are deflecting plots to be overthrown, managing rumors, gossip, and possible death threats or hits, and developing mental and physical illnesses while others may be looking to take over as boss. Unfortunately, some activists and politicians literally act like the mob, through threats and intimidation.

Maybe if the activist is exceptional and lucky, a park or building may be named after him or her. Many activists are easily forgotten and their work many times is taken for granted by future leaders/activists.

An activist might as well have gone into Mixed Martial Arts — there is more money and glory in getting beaten to a pulp. You have to be a masochist to be a mixed martial artist or better yet, a full time activist.

Chapter Three

Media as Advocacy Tool — Organizing Press Conferences and Writing Columns

Why write a book about becoming an activist? To share some useful information about how it is done. Take media coverage, for example. When I got hired with the California League of Conservation Voters, one of the first forums we conducted was in the poor area of Pico-Union to discuss voter education and environmental issues. Of course, the older activists from other non-profits had me organize the whole event. I did outreach and wrote my first press release. On purpose, the other activists had me speak at the end of the event when everyone was gone, including the media. Of course, they wanted to be the heroes and protagonists, and use a young lad to do the work for them. Boy do we learn from hard lessons. I guess it's called paying your dues. Algunos dicen, *"tienes que sudar la camiseta."* I remember showing a video from the National Association of Latino Elected and Appointed Officials (NALEO) on the importance of voting, but only a few audience members were left. I thought, so this is how it works — the older established activists use the younger activists. Not very good role models to emulate. But then again, we informed over one hundred new voters in a neglected area. That was fulfilling. Activists usually have to find or create a silver lining — to remain hopeful and optimistic.

Along the way, I learned the ABC's of writing a news release — the who, what, where, why, and when. You paint a picture that will make the news assignment desk want to cover your event, by offering useful information, plus strong visuals for television, newspaper, or Internet photographs.

During the same time, I helped to establish (on a minimal level) a new Salvadoran American organization, which eventually became the Salvadoran

American Leadership and Education Fund (SALEF). My good friend, may
he rest in peace now, Jesse J. Linares, did the first story regarding this
organization. We were very proud to be profiled in *La Opinion* newspaper.
That was the first time that I was cited in a newspaper article. Thanks to
Carlos Vaquerano for recruiting me to help, on a small scale, to establish
SALEF, which helps thousands of Central American/Latino students through
social service programs and scholarships.

I began working for the California League of Conservation Voters
(CLCV). I took some UCLA Extension courses around that time, that were
extremely useful, and I thoroughly enjoyed a big university campus atmos-
phere. At the California League of Conservation Voters (CLCV) I learned
how to write newspaper columns and the ins and outs of politics. David
Allgood was a great mentor and is an effective environmental activist. He is
knowledgeable, practical, and gets things done. David has helped to shape
monumental environmental protection legislation.

While working at CLCV, I published my first column in 1996 for *La
Opinion.* When the editor called me and said it would be published, I was
shocked. Then, they wanted to pay me for my second column. I was amazed,
why should I get paid to do something that I enjoyed? I got hooked and the
writing bug hit me hard. I wanted to write and write, publish columns.

At first I was not too secure in my writing abilities. When you grow up in
South Central, it is easy to fall through the cracks by not learning how to read
and write correctly. Many prison inmates do not know how to read and write.
I went to some of the most underperforming public schools in Los Angeles. I
started learning to read and write in Spanish, and in third grade I had to
switch to English, which put me behind. But as a child, I always loved books.
I would go to the library a lot after school. I would confuse the librarian,
since I was there so often to read and check out books. One time she asked
me, "Where is your family from?" And for some reason, I said "England." I
was in first grade, enthralled by wrestling, and I had just met a British
wrestler at the Shrine Auditorium. Maybe that is why I said it, or perhaps I
just wanted to fit in, since the librarian looked British and I liked the British
flag at that time. The silly things that children say and do to be accepted. The
worst part is that in middle school I would claim that George Michael was
my cousin. LOL.

But, back to writing and media. You had to read and write every day if
you wanted interesting and fresh press releases or columns, and effective e-
mails. Even people from the ghetto can become fine writers — after all, we
certainly have vivid memories to draw from. James Baldwin did a wonderful
job of depicting the pain and suffering of the U.S. Black community during
the 1950's and 1960's. He wanted to share the story of the poor, and painted
a realistic and powerful picture. He was bold and eloquent. And he was angry
to have lived and witnessed so many injustices.

Poverty is no foreign concept to kids who grow up in the ghettos of the United States. We did not go through an economic recession; we were born into an economic depression. Chronic economic depression. Jobs, what jobs?

Jobs never arrive in the ghetto; they left long ago, when U.S. corporations decided to relocate overseas to get cheap labor, to be able to violate environmental laws, and to avoid paying taxes. What a grand deal. The owners and shareholders have made a ton in profits, but the unemployed people back home are the ones who have suffered, and are left out in the cold.

Again, what are the seasoned activists doing to bring back the jobs or to create jobs? We have to blame someone and it is easy to blame the activists. Some darn troublemakers. Can't they just leave the poor politicians alone? No criticism allowed, or funds for the non-profits will be taken away. Some politicians begin to think that they are God — all knowing, all powerful. Just like the doctors or surgeons with a scalpel, who think "I can save your life or kill you if I want to." They may come up with contracts to begin charging you to use public streets, or force you to pay a maintenance fee where your non-profit is located. They may try to blackmail and intimidate you so that you will not dare challenge them. But you have a choice — to continue advocating or to sell out.

Remember, when you become proficient in writing those press releases — you must choose between being a team player or an activist who is on the side of the poor people. You can prepare and fax that news release about how beautiful and wonderful everything is, or denounce it when that coach savagely beats up a poor, skinny kid at a public high school. You have to report such an incident to the police. That will cost you many friends and you will not get awards. You may mainly gain criticism and enemies. You may not be able to sleep well at night due to the external pressures, but your conscience will be free for not selling your soul to the highest bidder. Just stay away from the devil's pleasures: alcohol and drugs. It will fuck you up. (Pardon my French vocabulary, but I do have French genes. Not British. Some Salvadoran and Hungarian too. Two conquered countries with much historic violence, but this past is part of why I want to create change.)

Communications 101: if you want to get attention, organize a press conference. If you want to get the Mayor's attention — just like we did during the Democratic National Convention held at the Los Angeles Convention Center — then do a press conference and have some activist say that the Mayor does not care about poor people. Most likely he or she will flip and cuss out those damn activists. He or she will say, "I do care about poor people — I was poor once, or my family was." How many candidates who run for office like to beef up their struggles as working class people — whether they were or not — trying to get the vote from the poor masses? They will even claim to have been suffering busboys. Also, instead of saying one is a millionaire, you have to downplay it and say you are part of the 99%.

Hey, there is nothing wrong with being part of the 1% as long as you care about the poor and give back somehow. A few individuals that come to mind who have done much advocacy and have made major public policy changes, through their philanthropy, are multi-millionaire's Molly Munger from the Advancement Project and George Soros, through the Soros Foundation. To some Soros is a hero, and to others he is not.

Getting back to media. How to organize a press conference: Select a good location, good parking, get other colleagues and experts to join you, e-mail and fax the press release, call media, and then moderate the press conference. Answer questions accurately and honestly. Then conclude, give material to reporters, and have spokespeople available to make a statement or do one-on-one interviews. Pray for the best.

That evening, monitor the news media and in the morning watch the local television news and read the newspapers online to see if you were successful in getting positive media coverage. Then if you have time, celebrate a little with your colleagues and allies. Having humor and time to celebrate the victories is important — otherwise you will become bitter, angry, frustrated, and grumpy. And who wants a grumpy or moody boyfriend or girlfriend? Especially one that gets home angry, and buys some booze to numb the annoying voices. Not a good idea. Therefore, the message is — don't go there. Avoid the alcohol and drugs at all costs. Even if you have to go to rehab. If someone else is down and out, try to help them by getting them to admit that they have a problem. Not to you necessarily, but try to be there for that suffering person, and try not to be judgmental about the pain of an addict. Also, avoid destructive personal/romantic relationships — of course, it's easier said than done. Oscar De La Hoya, former world boxing champion, is a good example that rehab is possible, and that one can turn his life around for the better. Oscar has sent a positive message, and continues to be a good role model, who has admitted his weaknesses and faults. He is now creating opportunities for up-and-coming young boxers, and gives back to his own community, particularly to White Memorial Hospital. He is especially interested in donating to cancer research since his mother passed away due to cancer.

Back to the subject of organizing. Do not crave media attention or coverage just for the hell of it. Organizing and implementing a press conference is serious business. Thousands or even millions of people may see or hear your message via television, radio, newspaper, or Internet. Preparing a responsible message is very important, and never lie to the media or they will get you back sooner or later. If you become a shallow, superficial activist, the community and media will begin to sniff the bullshit. If you are in it for real — you have to be the real deal, otherwise you are only lying to yourself and the community. Also, if you have press conferences that really have no purpose and substance then the media may stop showing up. Najee Ali is a good example. He exaggerated that he had created a truce between African-American and Latino gang members in the South Bay area. When the international media showed up, Najee had no local gang members present, and the media was asking *"where are the gang members that supposedly signed the truce?*

Another method of media or communications advocacy is via writing and the arts. It can be through social networks, blogs, Twitter, or by writing books, poetry, music, or by creating documentaries. Or through theater — like Ric Salinas, Richard Montoya, and Herbert Siguenza from Culture Clash.

Activists tend to be kindred spirits with artists and writers. Look at all of the great protest singers from the 1960's such as Bob Dylan, Joan Baez, and many others who helped to revolutionize social movements through the power of music. John Lennon told *Rolling Stone* magazine: "I've never claimed divinity or purity of soul. I only put out songs and answer questions as honestly as I can" (Rolling Stone, 2012, p. 7). Another protest singer and activist, is the much-less-famous Sixto Rodriguez, who finally obtained well-deserved attention through the documentary *Searching for Sugarman.* This excellent documentary recounts the life of Rodriguez, who recorded and released two amazing albums in the early 1970's, but did not get the attention or commercial success that he deserved. However, he became bigger than Elvis Presley in South Africa. The anti-apartheid movement adopted Rodriguez' albums as their anthems in fighting for social justice. The documentary provides a glimpse into Rodriguez and his amazing life. He has lived in Detroit, Michigan, and has actually run for city council and mayor. He did not earn the money that he deserved from his albums. He has lived a humble life, and has been working in construction for decades. When he finally did have the opportunity to visit South Africa, he was a received as a world-class hero. It is truly an inspirational story of struggle, perseverance, and commitment to social activism.

Look at the poets who gather in basements, cafes, libraries, or anywhere where they can share and recite their radical and innovative poetry. Edward Gonzalez recently decided to become a broke activist by documenting the Salvadoran American experience through his film titled *Words of Revolution.* He profiles young, up-and-coming Hip Hop artists, and writers of history and politics, who are making a difference through their music. Professors and teachers can be powerful activists, since they get to influence and motivate thousands of students. Sal Castro and Don White are great examples of that. Do young students know who they were? Sal Castro helped to lead the Chicano student walk-outs of 1968, and Don White was a leading activist in the Salvadoran solidarity movement. Don was a leader of the Committee in Solidarity with the People of El Salvador (CISPES). He was a true activist that was present at every protest and march. He was also a very effective public school teacher. Of course, conservatives will say that activists like Sal and Don were poisoning the minds of youth through teaching social justice movements and ethnic studies. The FBI did, in fact. monitor and infiltrate CISPES in the 1980's. Their offices were broken into, bugs were placed, and government informants were hired to destroy CISPES. In the 1980's, sympathizers of leftist movements in Latin America were, in fact, seen as a national threat, and many times they were labeled as terrorist supporters. Sometimes our U.S. Constitutional rights are trampled on, and/or ignored, and certain activists or literature if purposely banned.

It is a tragedy that Arizona has purposely chosen to ban ethnic books because some feel it is a threat to the status quo and mainstream way of thinking. Ironically, my first book, *Hope in Times of Darkness: A Salvadoran American Experience,* is not widely available in Arizona, but it is now available in China — a Communist country. A Democracy must embrace different points of views and thought. Freedom of expression is a precious right under our U.S. Constitution.

Communication channels can help prevent violence, or sometimes may even provoke violence. For example, the recent anti-Muslim documentary filmed in Duarte and Santa Clarita, California, then uploaded to YouTube, caused much chaos and violence in Libya, Egypt and other countries. It is a good example of irresponsible actions by individuals, who then distanced themselves from the negative reactions the film caused throughout the world. This documentary opened the door for terrorists to take action, and justify the destruction and murders of innocent victims.

Documentaries do play a key role in our society — similar, in some ways, to the manner in which newspapers influence and inform readers. Each newspaper needs to fact check, and be objective, professional, and reliable in its journalism coverage.

For example, a local newspaper published a story with the headline, *El Centro de Accion Social gets anti-violence grant: Local group to look at gangs, domestic violence and police clashes in the San Gabriel Valley.*

It seems to me that the reporter or editor did not thoroughly read the grant work plan that I faxed to them. El Centro de Accion Social did not obtain the grant due to the tragedy of Kendrec McDade, who was fatally shot by Pasadena Police officers. In fact, it was fatal shootings by the Anaheim police that influenced me to begin writing the grant.

As for the sub headline, *"Local group to look at gangs, domestic violence and police clashes in the San Gabriel Valley,"* the grant was not intended to do gang intervention, or focus on domestic violence issues. The intent of the project was to analyze the symptoms that lead to violence and discuss what we can do to collaborate on policy and systematic changes to help prevent and reduce violence in our society. Partnerships were developed with key organizations.

The article made it seem as if we took advantage of a tragedy to obtain a grant. I don't know what kind of questions or communication the reporter had with the Pasadena Police Department spokesperson, but the context of the questions and the way they are posed have an impact on how the person being interviewed responds. Reporters can be subjective in their choice of questions, and editors can influence how a story is read by the headline they write.

Many times human beings make assumptions without fact checking, doing research, or actually reading background material or reports. Sometimes reporters are on deadline and are rushed to get the story out. Sometimes they miss key information, misquote someone, or get a little too creative. Also, an interviewee should be prepared, and should take care with the information provided and statements made.

I am a strong supporter and advocate of freedom of expression and freedom of the press. We have to cherish and protect our U.S. Constitutional rights. I am glad that we have quality newspapers, but they need to stay responsible in their reporting.

El Centro de Accion Social has been working on issues of violence prevention for many years now. We did obtain a multi-year grant ($172,116) for 2008-2010 from The California Endowment titled Student Advocacy Project, to support a student-led advocacy effort to reduce violence and promote prevention strategies in middle and high schools in the Pasadena/Altadena area. Our project benefited countless students and community members. Our students became Peace Ambassadors. They promoted non-violence in their schools and communities, created newsletters, created and conducted a survey, and formally presented before the Pasadena Unified School District (PUSD). Our students gained confidence, improved their self-esteem, and learned public skills.

With the recent fatal police shootings of unarmed minority youth throughout Los Angeles County, I felt that it was essential to help reduce violence and prevent future fatal police-related shootings. We saw the deadly shootings in Anaheim, the death of a young Asian male in El Monte, who was choked to death by a local police officer, and the fatal beating of Kelly Thomas by Fullerton police officers.

El Centro's intent is to develop a collaboration that will include representatives from school districts, police departments, city officials, elected officials, community groups, and other interested individuals who want to work toward reducing violence.

It is not an easy task, but El Centro feels compelled to tackle some of our society's tough issues to help create safer communities for everyone. We could easily just focus on offering after-school tutoring programs and social services for our senior citizens. But we choose to take on broader responsibilities to create community change.

I received a phone call from Kendrec McDade's mother, who wanted to know if we received the grant due to Kendrec McDade's tragedy. I explained that our intent is to work together to help prevent future tragedies. I was personally upset that Kendrec McDade was fatally shot by the Pasadena Police Department. They will have to do a lot more work to rebuild trust within the African American and Latino communities, especially in North-west Pasadena and cities such as Fullerton and Anaheim. Only a father or mother who has lost a child to violence knows the pain, that deep pain that never goes away.

Ultimately, we must ask our local papers to be fair, objective, and professional in their reporting. It is our community. It is everyone's responsibility to work towards peace, justice, and non-violence. Let us honor and respect the memory of Kendrec McDade.

Chapter Four

Raising Money

Foundations, Government Grants, Fundraisers, and
Asking the Community You Serve to Give Back

Overall, raising money for non-profits is one of the key measures of being successful in implementing good social service programs. Of course, some non-profits are money raising machines but they have lost a sense of activism and advocacy. They have become very comfortable in having multi-million dollar budgets. Just like bureaucracies, who sometimes are simply bloated, some non-profits get so much government funding that they create random positions.

Being realistic, you can protest, demand, shout and scream, do sit-ins, and marches, but if you cannot raise money, that poor non-profit will not survive. Raising money is an art that can be learned. It is not easy, but it is possible. When I took over El Centro de Accion Social in Pasadena on December 12, 2005 I did not have much experience in raising money or writing grants. But I was motivated. My first big challenge was to write and prepare the Community Development Block Grant (CDBG) grant proposals. This was a lot of paperwork and bureaucracy to deal with for limited, yet essential funds to run our programs. We got this money from the Department of Housing and Urban Development (HUD) to help low income communities. Is it worth it? Yes. I'm sure the youth and senior citizens who benefit would agree. Our senior citizens continue to receive free health workshops provided by Kaiser Permanente and Huntington Memorial Hospital. They continue to learn English, they are becoming U.S. Citizens, and we provide some field trips.

It is our taxpayer money and we want it to be invested in the community, especially in the poor neglected areas of Pasadena and Altadena. But it is sad that we have to make so much noise to get such a small amount of money.

27

California Governor Jerry Brown decided to do away with Community Redevelopment Agencies, since he felt that the money was not going to revitalize blighted areas. The funds seemed to be channeled in other directions. Some developers, consultants, and special interest groups became wealthy through CRA contracts.

It is also important to be vigilant about how Federal money is received and spent by local city governments. Poor communities must make noise in order to be heard and taken into account. Otherwise, the money is usually used to build sophisticated new buildings, renovate stadiums, and complete the pet projects that are near and dear to certain elected officials. We must make sure that local community members are truly hired to work on construction jobs. Otherwise the jobs are simply given to friends of the elected officials, contractors, and insiders.

The cities of Bell, Maywood, and Vernon are good examples of unaccountability and systematic corruption at the local level. Investigations have taken place and let's continue to pray that new leadership will emerge and make sure that taxpayer money is used appropriately.

If your non-profit begins to receive large grants and begins to focus on doing regional, collaborative work, a lot of haters will come out of the woodwork. They will start making up rumors, gossips, and criticizing. Let's ask these haters to roll up their sleeves and start working for real instead of just talking smack. They are the first to make fun or try to destroy someone's character. But they have to look themselves in the mirror and face their own shortcomings and sins. If you are a sinner, then don't throw rocks to hurt others. Stop criticizing and get to work to make social change. Yes, I am ranting and raving, but we are all entitled to our own opinion. It is empowering to be able to speak our minds, but of course in a responsible manner, since words (written or spoken) do have a tremendous impact.

Our blessings in disguise have been foundations. It is challenging to maintain relationships with foundations because of changing leadership and evolving funding guidelines or priorities. One of the most challenging aspects is to obtain grants that last two or three years, rather than just one year. And don't forget to do your grant reports correctly if you want to get funded again.

Thank goodness for the corporations and wealthy millionaires and billionaires who help to create and establish foundations. They are the oxygen that keep many non-profits going. I have to give some credit to Henry Ford and the Ford Foundation. They have been a key source of funding for organizations such as the Mexican American Legal Defense and Education Fund (MALDEF). Also, the Mexican American Opportunity Foundation has been fortunate to have received federal funding for decades, to create jobs, provide child care, and other social services. MAOF is one of the biggest Latino non-profits in the United States with a budget of over $60 million and they employ over 600 staff members (part time and full time), throughout California and other states. Nonetheless, in today's tough economy, foundations are giving less money to non-profits and the process has become more competitive.

Most foundations require financial statements, audits, and 990's, to see which non-profits are responsible with their funds. Audits reassure donors that the non-profits they support are healthy, and that their money is being used appropriately. You obtain and review a non-profit's finances at Guidestar.com. They offer thorough information and a seal of approval. This is a good tool to show transparency. Many times it also boils down to the reputation of the Executive Director and Board members. Donors and foundations will become familiar with non-profits' Executive Directors and board members. Relationships are key but they do not necessarily determine if a non-profit will receive a grant. Foundation committees are often created to evaluate the merits of a grant proposal. This creates a more objective process. However, I have to point out that a California Latino legislator at one point proposed legislation that would have forced foundations to provide private information, to see how minority groups are being under-funded. The legislation sought to remedy this disparity, but the foundations soon agreed to begin to include minority non-profits in their pool of applicants. It is a sad statement when state legislation is almost necessary for foundations to provide funding to minority non-profits. Many times, certain profiles or stereotypes may persist when a minority non-profit applies for funding. Sometimes they may be perceived as not as trustworthy as well-known and established non-profits such as the YMCA, Boys & Girls Club of America, and United Way.

Non-profits such as El Centro de Accion Social have had to work very hard to establish themselves as a legitimate non-profit. They may not have multi-million dollar budgets, but they are good stewards and make a major impact in helping the poor with limited resources. Sometimes the smaller non-profits do more with less. Many national non-profits receive grants in the millions of dollar. Sometimes they mainly see their role as creating positions and spending the money, when it fact, it is not about spending the money, but making sure that they can continue to raise more money in order to continue the programs on a long-term basis.

Chapter Five

Three Well-Known and
Well-Established Non-Profits

I will analyze three of the oldest Latino non-profit organizations in Los Angeles to provide some case studies and specific examples of successful advocacy work: El Centro de Accion Social, founded in 1968; the Mexican American Legal Defense and Educational Fund (MALDEF) established the same year; and the Mexican American Opportunity Foundation, created in 1963.

El Centro de Accion Social (The Center for Social Action) was established over 45 years ago in Pasadena. It is now the oldest and largest Latino based non-profit in the San Gabriel Valley area. It was founded to empower the low-income Latino community of Pasadena, which was small, yet growing in 1968. Mexican American/Latino parents wanted to provide after-school tutoring for their children, to help them succeed in the United States.

At the request of a few community activists, the City of Pasadena provided a small building in Central Park, which was used for translation services, referrals to various aid agencies and other help the Latino community needed.

The organization continued to expand its programs and assistance to the community, and in the 1970s "Summer School in the Park" was developed. This after-school program offered summer classes, breakfast and lunch, and field trips for low-income students from the Pasadena Unified School District.

El Centro began to tackle issues that were controversial, but ultimately its actions have improved the lives of countless individuals. El Centro successfully sued the Pasadena Police Department, so it would promote and hire more minorities, and the City of Pasadena for changes in land development policy. Pasadena Latino activists did not want poor Latino community members to be displaced through high-priced housing prices. Taking on multi-million bureaucracies can be like David versus Goliath. Non-profits are usually at a disadvantaged since they cannot afford in house legal counsel.

The yellow building of El Centro, with its Aztec and Mayan murals, seems small, yet it is a powerful community-based organization that has stood the test of time, and is now 45 years old. In the 1990's it expanded its youth-education programs, and began serving low-income senior citizens in 1999. Now it provides youth education programs at John Muir High School, Washington Middle School, and Jefferson Elementary School. We continue to offer Summer School in the Park and we aid over 200 low-income senior citizens at our satellite location, Villa Parke Community Center. Many community members are strong supporters of El Centro de Accion Social. El Centro will continue to be a strong advocate for the needs of the Latino and non-Latino community of Pasadena and Altadena. El Centro is seen as the leading Latino advocacy group and has a legacy of being the voice of the community. It is not an easy task at all.

El Centro continues to promote the history and culture of the Latino community through our Day of the Dead *(Dia de los Muertos)*, Three Kings Day, Cesar Chavez Commemoration Day and Peace Walk, El Centro's Gloria Delaney Scholarship Fund for high school seniors, and its own successful annual fundraiser. The Pasadena Latino community has grown more diverse, and now includes individuals from many countries in Latin America.

We continue to focus on race relations, quality and equitable education, health care access and housing for low-income senior citizens, and peace and non-violence in our schools and community. Tony Massengale has been a close ally to El Centro de Accion Social. He is a well-known community organizer, who was a close friend of former Mayor Bill Bradley. Tony continues to organize community members as a full time senior staff member of the Los Angeles County Commission on Human Relations. He is passionate about social justice issues, and is a strong supporter of building bridges between African-American and Latinos.

El Centro de Accion Social remains a vibrant and powerful community-based organization, receiving funding from the federal government, foundations, corporations, and individual donors. We continue to have strong partnerships with the City of Pasadena, Pasadena Unified School District, Pasadena Police Department and the Pasadena Fire Department, though maintaining independence and offering advocacy for the community. It has evolved as an institution that has helped generations of families, and continues to develop key partnerships on many social issues. The community relies on El Centro to provide leadership on social justice issues. We also hold an annual fundraising event honoring key individuals who have improved our society tremendously. Many are unsung heroes and activists who have done a lot of community work under the radar.

One is 85-year-old Manuel Torres Contreras; he is the President of the Pasadena Mexican American History Association. Better known as Manny throughout Pasadena, he was born December 24, 1927 in Pasadena, to Angel Contreras and Juana Torres Contreras, one of five brothers and three sisters. He began Garfield Elementary School in 1934, graduated from McKinley Junior High School in 1940, and then attended Pasadena Junior College. He enlisted in the U.S. Coast Guard and served from 1945 to 1947. He majored in Civil Engineering and graduated from Pasadena City College in 1948.

Manny's professional work included being a draftsman for the Amerada Petroleum Corporation in 1951, a social worker for the Pasadena Settlement Association. He was also hired as a Civil Engineer Assistant for the Los Angeles County Department of Engineering, where he served for 35 years, retiring in 1990.

Actively involved in the Boy Scouts of America, Manny also served as Vice President of the L.A. County Chicano Employees Association, and co-founded the Pasadena Uni-Vets Club, the Pasadena Scholarship Committee for Mexican Americans, and the Pasadena Mexican American History Association.

Manny is a humble yet charismatic individual who has always cared for others and who actively promoted the culture and history of Mexican Americans. He endured much discrimination, evidenced by not being promoted within the Los Angeles County system, even though he scored very high on promotional tests and interviews. Manny persevered anyway. He witnessed first-hand how unjust federal laws kept various communities separated within Pasadena. Equal but separate was the law of the land, and Mexican Americans had to attend segregated schools, churches, and other institutions. Manny attended Our Lady of Guadalupe church and even served as an altar boy. He has an innate respect for, and pride in his heritage. Even in times of discrimination, he did not deny his roots. He served his country proudly in the U.S. Coast Guard, and has a kind heart and a sense for justice. For decades he has worked to improve the lives of Latinos and non-Latinos in Pasadena. Even at 85 years old, he remains active, but has not sought the limelight. One of his great memories was when he gave a speech as a student about Cinco de Mayo. His mother bought him a suit and his speech made her very proud. In countless photographs, Manny has captured the history of Pasadena.

Manny serves as a role model to thousands of people, with a powerful smile and a kind and generous heart. The community organizations he helped to establish have served many people for decades — providing safety nets for the poor. There are others like Manny. Take Tecumseh Shackelford (Shack), who founded the Mentoring and Partnership for Youth Development (MPYD) mentorship program at John Muir High School. He is a retired volunteer, who cares very much about helping youth to succeed. So does

Jaylene Moseley, President of the Flintridge Center. The center has raised millions of dollars to help the most needy in Pasadena and Altadena. Jaylene is very successful and financially well off, and she chooses to give back to the community. Her example should be emulated by other wealthy individuals. The 1% of wealthiest Americans can and should give back to the most needy. This would create a more equitable and fair society. Jaylene truly believes that each student, regardless of their economic status, can academically succeed.

Non-profits have historically served as safety valves in our society, and in many cases help to prevent social riots and social upheaval from occurring. Corporations in an ingenious manner established foundations that would eventually give money to non-profits, which are legally registered as 501 (c) 3s. They are incorporated, but under federal and state laws, individuals or corporations who donate money to non-profits are eligible to receive a tax break. This is an incentive for individuals to support community-based organizations (non-profits) that are doing community work and are good stewards of funds.

Some of the first American multi-millionaires, such as Andrew W. Mellon and John D. Rockefeller, established very powerful foundations that now have endowments in the billions of dollars. They wanted to give money and to also establish universities, hospitals, libraries, and other institutions that would make positive social contributions and change. They were visionaries who recognized that they would not be able to spend their vast amounts of wealth. Instead, they chose to carry on their names and legacies through their giving.

The official website of the Andrew W. Mellon Foundation states "Our grant-making philosophy is to build, strengthen and sustain institutions and their core capacities, rather than be a source for narrowly-defined projects. As such, we develop thoughtful, long-term collaborations with grant recipients and invest sufficient funds for an extended period to accomplish the purpose at hand and achieve meaningful results."

The human ego is so powerful that many of these individuals wanted buildings to be named after them, in order for their legacies and memories to continue after death. Even today billionaires such as Eli Broad are willing to provide tens or hundreds of millions of dollars to certain non-profits that agree to place his wife's name or his name on the building. Bill Gates also loved to provide funds for health research and other innovative and breakthrough non- profits. He received tremendous amounts of press coverage for the philanthropic work by the Melinda and Bill Gates Foundation.

Most non-profits face a tremendous challenge in raising enough funds to continue offering vital programs and services, and boards of directors often are missing in action when it comes to raising funds. "For a variety of reasons, board members commonly hate to ask for money. Even when they are cajoled into saying they will do it, it is not unusual to find that they underperform their commitments. After all the videos on 'teaching your board to fundraise' and all the consultants and all the classes — it is still the rare board that raises any significant portion of the dollars the organization brings in," (Gottlieb, 2008).

Since underperforming and not-so-committed boards are a main reason why so many non-profits are unable to raise enough funds, the burden is usually placed on the Executive Director. If the money is raised, everyone takes credit, but if it isn't, then the board considers replacing an "underperforming" Executive Director or Chief Executive Officer (CEO). Many individuals join boards to simply place their name on the letterhead and to feel important. That does not really contribute to and empower an organization. Also, the role of board member is not to denigrate or personally attack the Executive Director, but is to uplift and strengthen the organization, and help carry out the mission. Of course, the role of board members is to oversee the performance of executive directors, and yes, sometimes a board can respectfully criticize, but it is best when it is done in a professional manner. Boards ultimately have the right to replace Executive Directors who engage in illegal activities, or who are not able to raise enough funds.

"Many non-profit members or donors strongly object to thinking of their nonprofit as a business. That word is too closely linked with the evils of a profit-driven corporate world, where many must work for pay. They volunteer, in part, to escape that world and to work for nobler cause" (Wilcox, 2006). This sentiment helps to explain why some board members believe they do not need to fundraise, because they already contribute their time and their mere presence. Unfortunately, board members often serve for the wrong reasons.

In terms of everyday operations and management of staff, dealing with a board, and balancing a budget, running a non-profit is like running a business. The same responsibilities fall on an Executive Director, whether it is a $500,000 operation or a multi-million dollar operation. The dominant mindset is that Executive Directors should be compensated based on the size of the non-profit's budget, but the reality is that smaller non-profits have a hard time competing against the larger ones, which — because of their corporate boards, support from elected officials, and extensive fundraising departments whose directors are paid well over $100,000 a year — tend to prevail in fundraising. Many times these larger non-profits attract corporate management leaders who want to have more inroads in the community and to project the image that they are fulfilling their community philanthropic responsibility.

That is wonderful if board members can put the interest of the non-profit first, and deliver funds that empower the non-profit with no strings attached. Hidden agendas by certain board members can actually injure the reputation or focus of a community organization. For example, sometimes individuals are interested in joining boards because they wish to run for political office or to further expand the contacts, network, and contracts of their businesses.

In today's tough economy, El Centro de Accion Social has to compete with many other organizations for scarce resources. It is a healthy competition — keeping El Centro vibrant and innovative. Most non-profits are going to the same foundations and corporations seeking support, and even the large non-profits such as MALDEF and MAOF are applying for smaller grants in order to keep their budgets balanced. Although this creates more competition for smaller non-profits, such as El Centro de Accion Social, it helps to motivate the staff to continually raise funds. It is like a marathon that takes place every year. Seeking grants from foundations is a never ending process.

MALDEF's budget is in the range of $6 million per year and MAOF's is $60 million per year. MALDEF was fortunate to receive a $1 million seed grant from the Ford Foundation. Also, a co-founder of MEChA, Luis Nogales, has become a great champion and advocate for MALDEF. In 2001, Luis and his wife donated $1 million to MALDEF for immigrants' rights work. Luis Nogales is an example of a powerful individual who had humble beginnings; starting as a farm worker in Calexico, eventually obtaining his education at San Diego State University and Stanford University. Now he has a law degree, sits on the boards of powerful corporations, and formerly was President of Univision and CEO of United Press International (UPI). Luis is a good example that you can become a powerful corporate insider without having to deny your roots or forgetting your history. He has used his intelligence, wealth, connections, and knowledge to empower non-profits too.

MALDEF has grown tremendously, and many corporations tend to donate since they do not want to get targeted or sued by MALDEF's attorney. It is interesting how power works and it is important to analyze who sits on the boards of these non-profits. If only we could get other Latino/Latina multimillionaires to give back to their own communities. That would be something. Many will claim that they already do, but is it enough since the needs are so great. I see the names of the top 100 most influential Latinos/as on the cover of certain magazines and I wonder if they equate success merely with material wealth and influential corporate or government positions. I wonder if one day anyone will acknowledge the 100 most knowledgeable and successful Latino/a (Hispanic) activists in the United States.

Even though El Centro is much smaller in size and its main focus is local issues, it remains competitive in terms of name recognition among non-profits because it is located in Pasadena (San Gabriel Valley area), which usually is not served by the Los Angeles-based MALDEF and MAOF. It would be nice if someday MALDEF would also decide to become more involved in the San Gabriel Valley area. Some Pasadena activists have in the past approached MALDEF seeking help, but they have not obtained much support. In order for non-profits to remain effective not just at the elite policy level and ivory legal halls, they must include grassroots campaigns and we must remind them to not forget their social justice roots. It is easy for certain non-profits to be coopted by Boards that predominantly include the self-interests of various corporations. Non-profits must remain vigilant to remain financially, politically independent, in order to not be bought or beholden to political favors.

MALDEF states its mission as "the nation's leading Latino legal civil rights organization. Often described as the 'law firm of the Latino community,' MALDEF promotes social change through advocacy, communications, community education, and litigation in the areas of education, employment, immigrant rights, and political access." Some non-profits believe they are so large and influential that they do not have time to get involved in local politics or policy issues. They would rather take on cases that have national impact. Sometimes they may develop a hierarchical attitude and discount the role of small non-profits. Certain Executive Directors, CEOs, and Presidents of major non-profit may develop an elitist attitude and begin to feel superior to the smaller non-profits. Many times they do not bother to respond to e-mails or phone calls, unless of course if they feel that they can obtain a major donation or gain political access, then they will return phone calls. Just remember, *what goes around comes around* — or better yet, *what you sow is what you reap.*

MAOF's mission statement says "The Mexican American Opportunity Foundation (MAOF), the nation's largest Latino-serving social service organization, has been helping children and families in need since 1963," (MAOF official web site). We must be upfront to recognize that many non-profits Missions are not even known by the staff or board members. Sometimes Mission statements just sound good and are nice to put on a wall. The real mission of MALDEF, MAOF, and El Centro de Accion Social must be to not sell out and to remain true to their founding principles, which are usually idealistic yet very real. Fundamentally, the role of non-profits must be to help the most needy in our society. Non-profits should not be created for self-aggrandizement purposes, to obtain big paychecks, to dole out contracts, hire your friends as consultants, or be subservient to the interests and tantrums of self-serving politicians.

MALDEF and MAOF are much bigger non-profits than El Centro, although the roles and responsibilities of the Executive Director are the same. MALDEF and MAOF leaders have a bigger travel budget and can fly to other states and countries, as well as to national conferences, and to Washington D.C., to meet with members of the U.S. House of Representatives, the U.S. Senate, and the Executive branch. There is nothing wrong with that, and each Executive Director or CEO works very hard to attain a good salary. Y porque no? At least non-profit leaders are not getting those $20-$30 million salaries that many corporate CEOs get, whether they deserve it or not. As the Executive Director of El Centro, I've had to work very hard to convince the board to approve a budget for a trip to Washington D.C. When in the end I was able to obtain an $89,000 grant from the Department of Justice, it was well worth the small investment of travel and staying in a modest hotel. However, many stories have been documented in which Executive Directors and CEOs take advantage of their organizations and spend extravagantly on personal things such as elite cuisine, five-star hotels, limousines, and first class travel. Some "steal" thousands or millions of dollars to live the good life, by buying high-class golf memberships with the organization's money, and so much more. Some con artists who squirm their way into non-profits, say that they need these exclusive memberships to mix with the elite and to take their money. Some Executive Directors are so desperate in raising money — that they will hire consultants who often bleed the non-profit dry. This is unethical and there should be a department or website, where unethical consultants can be reported if they have engaged in illegal activities.

How sad that so many get away with it. Hopefully these thieves will be prosecuted and incarcerated, or forced to do community work — sweeping the streets, picking up trash, and cleaning graffiti.

Non-profits refer to the people that they serve as clients, community members, supporters. Some do not like to refer to them as "customers" since this implies that the non-profit is operating as a business, and the term "customer" demeans the value of the community being served.

At El Centro we refer to the individuals that we serve or help as youth or senior citizens. We address each person by name. Our job is to help the voiceless. Peter F. Druckner stated, "And then, the second rule, know your customers. Yes, I said *customers.*"(Druckner, 1990). He goes further by stating:

> So, the design of the right marketing strategy for the non-profit institution's service is the first basic strategy task: the non-profit institution needs market knowledge. It needs a marketing plan with specific objectives and goals. And it needs what I call marketing responsibility, which is to take one's customers seriously. Not saying, We know what's good for them, but, What are their values? How do I reach them? (Druckner, 1990)

El Centro agrees with Druckner that we do need to know our market, but the staff at El Centro prefers not to use the term customer. The majority of the staff are Latino/a and bilingual and are culturally sensitive to the needs of our community. It takes many years to build this communication, loyalty, and trust. We continually adapt to meet the needs of the community. For example, thousands of Asian immigrants have moved to Pasadena. We serve many Asian immigrants within our senior citizen program.

MALDEF serves a policy/legal role to defend the rights of the Latino community. They do class action lawsuits and have taken on, and won, monumental legal cases. Even though lately, we have not seen MALDEF become very involved in community affairs. MAOF deals directly with many community members that they serve through their Head Start programs, job training, and other activities. El Centro plays more of a grassroots role in dealing directly and face-to-face with community members that we help through our after school programs, summer school in the park, and senior citizen services offered at Villa Parke Community Center in Pasadena. Of course, it would be ideal to also have enough funds for an in-house civil rights attorney to help the community with legal cases. Many times immigrants are beaten and feel that they have not place to turn to. However, the Latino community is beginning to feel that El Centro has responded by conducting press conferences to denounce violence, whether the perpetrators are the police, gangs, or a high school coach. That is the role of a non-profit organization, to advocate for the needs of the community members that they serve. In 2006, El Centro de Accion Social joined forces with Pasadena's National Association for the Advancement of Colored People (NAACP) to denounce hate crimes and we asked the police department to prosecute the perpetrators under hate crime laws. Dozens of attacks were done against working-class Latino immigrants, with these physical attacks occurring for years and gang members acting with impunity. However, after El Centro and the NAACP made these injustices public, then most of the attacks ceased to occur. Key alliances are important in order to make solid progress. We cannot just afford to have coalitions/collaboratives where all they do is talk, talk, talk and philosophize. Actions speak louder than words. The needs of the community are so dramatic that non-profits should not just be talking about the problems, but actually be creating solutions.

El Centro de Accion Social was officially incorporated as a non-profit 501 c (3) in 1973 with the Secretary of State of California. Being officially incorporated as a non-profit for four decades demonstrates a legacy of longevity and financial responsibility. A few of the founders from the late 1960s and early 1970s are still very supportive, even though they are not directly or physically active. Many of the activists from the 1960s have passed away, while others are ill and cannot remain as involved as they once were. Still, their support helps to keep the legacy and uniqueness of El Centro alive. El Centro has deep roots and a long positive history in the community.

MALDEF and MAOF were also incorporated with the Secretary of State of California. All non-profits have to comply with rules and regulations of this office. We have to file 990 income tax reports, and non-profits with budgets over $500,000 must implement and conduct independent audits. El Centro pays $5,000 for an independent auditor to conduct an annual audit.

The State Attorney General's office role in regulating non-profits, includes making sure that they are legitimately established and non-fraudulent. Some non-profits do commit fraud and many are prosecuted if it can be proven that they have misappropriated or stolen funds. Ultimately, the Board of Directors is responsible for macromanaging and making sure that non-profit's staff and Executive Director are being responsible with funds. Board members are protected by insurance coverage, and their own personal assets are not in danger if a non-profit is sued or investigated. Ultimately, the staff is held accountable, and usually the Executive Director is asked to resign when scandals occur. If enough evidence is found, then the board can decide whether legal proceedings are advisable/appropriate.

It is important for the Board of Directors to be truly engaged in approving and reviewing organizational budgets, and for the Executive Director to feel comfortable being straightforward with the Board when deficits occur. "Budgetary slack or padding occurs when managers believe they are going to be evaluated on their performance relative to the budget. To ensure that they will achieve their budgeted figures and be rewarded, they budget revenues conservatively or exaggerate anticipated costs, or do both" (Harvard Business Essentials, 2002, p. 132). Illegal activities may occur when communication between the board and the Executive Director or CEO is poor. Internal oversight is key to making sure that non-profits are following the regulations, rules, and laws.

MALDEF, MAOF, and El Centro do not have labor unions representing the staff. However, non-profits are usually allies with organized labor since we serve similar constituencies, usually the disenfranchised and working class. But some non-profits do, in fact, have labor unions representing their staff, particularly non-profits in the medical field. For example, Clinica Romero, which has multi-million dollar budget and fifty to one hundred staff members, has a labor union to represent staff needs and labor rights. The Board of Directors had no choice but to accept the labor union.

The relationship has not been harmonious. Some staff have been upset at the Board of Directors due to budget cuts that led to massive lay-offs. A labor union representing the staff staged protests in front of the three Clinica Romero sites, including the home of the Board President.

A key role of non-profits in our society is to help the most disadvantaged, but in the process many non-profits divert from the mission of helping the most needy and engage in controversial and self-destructive activities.

We have heard countless cases of fraud-ridden corporations and banks. We know of WorldCom, Enron, and many others. But non-profits also get into trouble, and those who suffer the most are the people who desperately need the services and programs.

A controversial case that merits more analysis and attention is the non-profit Clinica Romero. This community-based organization was founded in the early 1980s to help Central American refugees with health and medical-care issues. I previously served on its Board of Directors. Clinica Romero grew from a small grass-roots community organization to a large, multi-million dollar non-profit institution with three locations and $10 million. Their organization is unusual, since most Central American non-profits have small budgets.

It may have grown too fast in order to keep up with the needs of the community. Also, it heavily relied on government support, which recently has drastically diminished.

In 2002, The UCLA Center for Civil Society conducted a research study titled *The Challenge of Meeting Social Needs in Los Angeles,* and it found that "nonprofit organizations in the human service field are partners of government rather than substitutes. They are organizations that need sustained public support, rather than a 'cheap' solution for reduction in government responsibility." Clinica Romero has definitely served a key role in helping thousands of individuals with medical care, but it definitely has taken a big hit due to the economic recession.

In frustration, accusations and rumors were made that the current Executive Director and President of the Board engaged in illicit activities (as in pilfering funds), and public protests were held to demand their resignations. However, we cannot forget that these were accusations and rumors. We must value the legal mantra that states "innocent until proven guilty."

Since the economic recession began, many employees had to be laid off, creating a lot of anger, despite the fact that Clinica Romero had a labor union that represented the staff.

Clinica Romero engaged in controversy, infighting, accusations, and lawsuits, temporarily lost its main purpose, which was to serve the poor communities that are desperate to receive medical care and medications at low costs.

Ultimately, the patients are the ones who suffered the most due to these conflicts. Yes, it is the responsibility of the Board of Directors to macromanage and to help make sure that the budget is balanced. However, the day-to-day operations are the responsibility of the executive director and he or she must hire competent and effective development and fundraising staff. However, the Executive Directors at Clinica Romero do not last long. It is a revolving door, continuing the chaos. A non-profit needs to hire a leader who will at least stick around for five years or more, to begin to make dents in improving the organization's budget, staff morale, delivery of programs/services. A Board should not hire Executive Directors who are looking for a quick buck and an opportunity to expand their resume. An Executive Director must be committed to stick around. Unfortunately, many do not stick around. Some are looking for the best big job opportunity that will pay more and they leave non-profits high and dry.

What Clinica Romero needed was a strategy to get their finances in order and to work together as a team. The remaining Board members, management staff, and labor union needed to be rational and focused on raising funds to help Clinica Romero to survive this turbulent period. It was easier to engage in destructive accusations than to roll up their sleeves and raise the funds needed to continue to offer vital health related services. The Executive Director that they hire should have management skills and not necessarily be a doctor. What Clinica needs is an effective administrator that knows about management, budgets, and how to motivate and inspire his or staff staff.

Clinica Romero represents so much for the Salvadoran and Central American community, since it carries the name of Archbishop Romero, who wanted the poor to be treated with dignity and respect. The Archbishop was murdered by death squads in 1980 while he was presiding over mass.

Archbishop Romero would be disappointed that Clinica Romero currently finds itself in controversy, and that people who are supposed to be progressives are fighting with each other and engaging in personal attacks.

All parties engaged in Clinica Romero's affairs must be held accountable by the community members that it serves. The future Board of Director members and the Executive Director must step up and raise the funds to help Clinica Romero to survive its critical economic challenges.

It would also be refreshing to see the angriest individuals get involved in helping to raise funds to help save Clinica Romero. There is no time for continual infighting and self-destructive actions.

Clinica Romero is bigger than controversies and protests — its role is to serve the neediest through health-care services. Archbishop Romero gave his life fighting for the poor. Since this non-profit chose to borrow Archbishop Romero's name — Clinica Romero must protect its reputation and integrity and must continue to serve the most needy.

Also, we have to recognize that significant infighting has occurred within the labor movement, but the AFL-CIO remains a force to be reckoned with, since they have over 16 million members throughout the United States. "In 2008, union membership grew by 428,000, increasing the percentage of union members in the workforce to 12.4 percent, up from 12.1 percent in 2007. Overall, 16.1 million workers carry union cards" (Hall, 2009).

Even though some labor unions have been accused of corruption and being affiliated with the mafia, most are legitimate and continue to fight for the rights of the average working-class family. Labor unions are ethnically diverse and they do raise millions of dollars through union membership dues. The members are generally happy to pay these dues in order to obtain legal and legitimate representation. Labor unions do in fact help to balance our democracy by providing a voice to millions of hard-working Americans. Maria Elena Durazo has been the Executive Secretary-Treasurer of the Los Angeles County Federation of Labor, AFL-CIO since 2006. She is a strong and committed labor leader who has been in the frontlines for decades. She is very powerful and can mobilize thousands of workers. Many businesses and corporations who refuse to allow unions are afraid of Maria Elena Durazo since they know that she is committed to social justice and relentless in community organizing efforts. Unions do in fact counterbalance the influence of corporations. Members of unions pay membership dues that help cover everyday expenses of union services and organizing. They have much influence since most unions are self-sustaining and responsible with how membership dues are utilized.

Some non-profits have developed and established a membership base. Members pay a yearly membership donation and the non-profit in return can produce more newsletters and can use the membership dues to help make payroll and to continue to grow the membership department. Some environmental organizations, such as the California League of Conservation Voters (CLCV), have developed a strong membership base and this provides much volunteer power. Many of their members are high-propensity voters who truly care about protecting the environment and voting for pro environmental candidates. Many times when you become a member of a non-profit you are pretty much trusting them with your donations. We expect these non-profits to use membership funds to not only help sustain the organization, but to actually make social impact. If they say that they will protect trees, then trees should be protected. If they say that bus diesel fumes are bad, then they should advocate and lobby to change laws that will protect the health of their members and non-members.

According to Drucker, "A business earns its money on its own. The money of the non-profit institution is not its own; it is held in trust for the donors. And the board is the guardian to make sure the money is used for the results for which it has been given. That, too, is part of the non-profit strategy" (Drucker, 1990). The internal ethical expectations of MALDEF, MAOF, and El Centro are very high, since the three are the oldest Latino non-profits in California. Also, the ethical expectations of its leaders are high and demanding. This does not mean that the Executive Director, staff, or Board members need to be perfect, but they do need high standards and a good moral gauge. The relationship between Board of Directors and staff must remain professional at all times.

El Centro has to deal with the demographic shifts in Pasadena. A growing percentage of the local population, close to 35%, is Latino, and demands on El Centro have grown. According to the 2012 Quality of Life Index, "there are geographic earning disparities within Pasadena. In the 91103 zip code, the median income was $44,358, compared to its southern neighbor, 91105, which has a median income of $91,587." The study also found that "Pasadena and Altadena have strong divide between public and private education. Though Los Angeles County only has a private school enrollment rate of around 8%, Pasadena and Altadena have much higher rates at 23.3% and 30.1%, respectively" (Quality of Life Index, 2012, p. 2).

MALDEF serves the millions of Latinos in California by winning major legal cases and helping to establish national case law. MAOF has programs throughout California, specifically in Los Angeles, Kern, Monterey, Santa Barbara, and Orange counties. Like El Centro, it serves mainly the low-income Latino community. El Centro also serves non-Latinos who seek our services. We help individuals from many countries throughout the world that include: Syria, Armenia, Malaysia, Taiwan, China, Korea, Mexico, Nicaragua, El Salvador, Colombia, and many other countries. We do not turn away anyone that needs our help. That is why our programs are very popular and effective.

El Centro de Accion Social started in 1968 as an activist organization, and evolved into a well-established, social-service type of non-profit. El Centro does focus on advocacy when necessary. In my capacity as executive director, we have advocated to obtain more funding to continue offering our social service programs that do benefit youth and senior citizens. We continue to advocate on behalf of our constituency for the City and the school district to support after school programs and violence prevention efforts. We advocate for the safety of our students, senior citizens, and we denounce when hate crimes occur. We advocate for the police department to treat minority community in a fair and respectful manner. We advocate for peace and to build coalitions. When necessary we refer community members to other non-profits where they can obtain different types of services such as food, clothing, mental health, and therapy.

MALDEF's culture is to be at the cutting edge of legal cases; their objectives are to win legal cases and to hopefully establish case law. MAOF offers social services to youth and provides job-training. It obtains tens of millions of dollars for its Head Start programs. They now have over 600 staff members and are expanding in other states to offer services there.

MAOF is a classic example of a community-based organization that mainly provides social services and programs. The Executive Director, staff, and Board do not necessarily get involve in social justice or advocacy struggles. They are program services organizations that fly under the radar even though their budget is in the $60 million range. Many non-profits abstain from making waves or creating noise since they simply want to continue obtaining millions of dollars from the federal government.

El Centro de Accion Social is stable even though we have to raise money on a daily basis to continue offering our programs. MALDEF and MAOF are on solid fundraising ground even though they too must continually raise funds. The economic crisis has hit non-profits very hard. Non-profits must now be more competitive, have leaner budgets, and rely on foundation grants in order to survive. Many corporations are not making profits like before and cannot afford to help as non-profits on the same scale they used to. Many non-profits that have lost government grants and contracts are now applying for grants from foundations, making the process more competitive. Also, many foundations have shrunken endowments since stock market shares have lost much value. Now the foundations are giving less to non-profits.

Yes, foundation endowments recently have been hard hit and individuals who traditionally give to charity have suffered financial reversals. But many nonprofits in their communities are in truly desperate straits. They have endured a triple whammy on the revenue side — donations, grants, and government support are all down — while community needs and demands for services have skyrocketed during the current economic crisis (Urban Institute web site, 2011).

The politics among non-profits are simply cutthroat. The economy has created a "survival of the fittest" mentality. MALDEF and MAOF have internal fundraising departments and their politics are tied to influential elected officials, attorneys, corporations, foundations and other donors. El Centro's strength has been its strong and consistent commitment of helping the poor in Pasadena. Through the decades, El Centro has fought many battles to bring about social change.

The technology of El Centro is simple and effective and has been upgraded to include a top-notch website, efficient computers, good software, and a social media networks via Facebook, Twitter, and e-mail.

MALDEF has a sophisticated technology since they deal with very sensitive legal matters and information. MAOF's technology is good and solid, but they need to do more outreach in order to inform more community members about the great services that they offer.

The stakeholders for El Centro are the youth, senior citizens, Board members, and donors. For MALDEF the stakeholders are the staff, board, people they serve, and their donors. The stakeholders for MAOF are the people they serve, board, staff, and donors.

The general management capacity of El Centro de Accion Social is stable. We have a small, dedicated and effective staff. The staff of El Centro are well educated and have a commitment towards social justice work. The key to good management for a non-profit is for its leadership not to micro manage: the board does not micro-manage the Executive Director and the Executive Director does not micro-manage the staff.

It is imperative for board members to know their roles and responsibilities and not overstep them. *Board source* published Ten Basic Responsibilities of Nonprofit Boards, clearly outlining the roles of board members. This information was provided to the board members of El Centro de Accion Social.

MALDEF's has a seasoned leader with Tom Saenz, who is an attorney with decades of experience in the non-profit world. He has served in other management capacities too. He was the chief counsel to former Mayor Antonio Villaraigosa. "Saenz has been one of Villaraigosa's closest advisors since taking the post in August 2005, recently serving as the mayor's lead representative in negotiations with city labor unions over salary and benefit concessions to help close the city's $530-million budget gap. And he helped to successfully defend a city ordinance that required hotels near Los Angeles International Airport to pay a 'living wage' to workers" (Willon, 2009, p. 1).

The Mexican American Opportunity Foundation (MAOF) was created by Donicio Morales, who was a nationally recognized civil rights leader. He left a legacy of caring for the poor and the voiceless. More than a decade ago, the board decided to recruit Martin Castro, who is very knowledgeable in running a non-profit and is adept with numbers and budget. He makes sure that the budget is balanced and that the Human Resources Department hires qualified individuals.

Martin Castro states:

> For over four decades, the Mexican American Opportunity Foundation (MAOF) has provided human services to underserved communities in California. From its humble beginnings in East Los Angeles, today our geographical service area includes seven California counties. It is a tradition that continues to be unmatched by any Latino non-profit service organization and supports the claim that MAOF is the largest Hispanic non-profit in the Country, as noted by Hispanic Business Magazine each of the last four years. From a well-established base of 28 licensed child-care and development centers serving 3,000 preschool children, to serving another 5,000 children in our Cal WORKS Program to help parents move from public assistance to gainful employment, to serving youths and adults with job training and job placement services, to providing senior citizens with a myriad of services in their golden years, MAOF serves well over 100,000 California residents each year (MAOF web site). MAOF continues to offer effective programs.

MALDEF and MAOF are in a league of their own but they do have to compete with other major national non-profits such as National Council of La Raza, League of United Latin American Citizens (LULAC), and National Association of Latino Elected and Appointed Officials (NALEO). They compete for corporate sponsorships and foundation grants. Since El Centro de Accion Social is local, we do not have to compete at the national level. However, we do compete with other local non-profits that seek the same funds that we do in order to continue in operation.

El Centro, MALDEF, and MAOF are strong, stable organizations that have proven that they have the capability to survive decades. MAOF does wonderful and expansive work, but needs to do a better job in providing information about the all of the wonderful work that they do and the major impact that they make in various communities. El Centro has a good communications capacity through their web-site, Facebook, e-mails, and direct mailing that keep community members informed of their activities and achievements. At MALDEF, MAOF, and El Centro, the board sets policy and the Executive Director or CEO must implement the strategies that are developed at board meetings or retreats.

The Board of Directors monitors whether strategic initiatives are being implemented. But it is the Executive Director or CEO of MALDEF, MAOF, and El Centro who needs to make sure the strategic plans are being implemented correctly and in a timely manner. The year-end foundation grant reports are essential and must be done correctly. Many Foundations require thorough reports that empirically prove that the funds did make a significant difference in the lives of the community members being served. Data and narrative reports must be provided describing how the grant was implemented, how programmatic goals were achieved, and how the funds were expended.

MALDEF has developed a sophisticated method of marketing its name brand among the well-educated in society, but the average working-class citizen would most likely not recognize or know what MALDEF stands for. Some would say that it needs to develop a grassroots marketing campaign. MAOF does a good job of marketing, but mainly among the community it serves. They need to do more media outreach. Most people are not familiar with MAOF's name or work. Since El Centro is a local non-profit, it is well known in the community, and Pasadena's high newspaper readership reinforce that recognition. Still, El Centro, just like other non-profits, needs to improve its marketing and outreach to keep the community informed. They all also need to keep developing website content, producing events and fundraisers, and making sure that day-to-day operations are running, with staff that coordinate the programs.

Research and development for the three non-profits includes identifying foundations, corporations, and donors, as well as viewing and visiting other programs. Non-profits must not become myopic. They have to learn from the successes and program models of other non-profits. MALDEF and MAOF have human resources departments. At El Centro, the Executive Director has to play the role of the Human Resources Director, by hiring and firing staff. The firing part is the least favorite role that an Executive Director must exercise. It can keep you awake at night.

Each non-profit has to follow the general accounting principles used in the state of California. Also, MALDEF, MAOF, and El Centro must develop an annual operating budget, and income and expense reports for the board. Each institution has an accountant that helps to manage the finances. Ultimately, it is the responsibility of the executive director or CEO to make sure that the budget is balanced. The Executive Director must be on top of the budget, or a deficit may develop.

Information systems for non-profits vary in size and quality; the budget determines how much is allocated for them. For example, MALDEF and MAOF spend tens of thousands of dollars in maintaining their information systems while El Centro seeks pro bono services from an IT expert. We pay him a small stipend.

The management and administration is set up in a hierarchical manner at MALDEF, MAOF, and El Centro. The Board of Directors sets macro policy and the Executive Director or CEO reports to the board. However, according to the Annenberg Foundation, the Board and the Executive Director should see each other professional partners, and the Executive Director should not be perceived as a "flunky" or puppet. It is essential for Executive Directors to understand their leadership roles, the power they hold, and ascertain whether they are doing things correctly and following professional management principles. Ideally, the President of the Board and the Executive Director are supposed to have good communication, trust, and loyalty to the non-profit.

MALDEF, MAOF, and El Centro have each existed for over four decades. Most of their social services and legal services are provided completely free of charge, which is pretty amazing given the state of the economy. Their employees are highly qualified and committed to helping the community. Most do not get paid extravagant salaries, but they provide excellent programs and services.

MALDEF has highly qualified attorneys that take on difficult cases and win. It also has a powerful development department that can raise millions of dollars, and a strong Board of Directors.

MAOF's strength is based on its solid work, access to federal money, strong board, and stable staff.

El Centro's strength is its 45 years' experience and service to the local community. Also, the staff is qualified and the Board is strong and stable.

A major problem for non-profits is the constant chase for money. However, MALDEF, MAOF, and El Centro have been around for so long that each institution already knows the process of applying for grants and seeking corporate support. But it is never easy work. MALDEF and MAOF are much better at obtaining corporate support since corporate leaders are well represented on their boards, as are well-known attorneys, and individuals who are politically connected at the state and national level.

El Centro has had a harder time obtaining big checks from corporations because we are local, but we are slowly improving in this realm.

What makes non-profits shaky is their reliance on foundation and government grants. These grants can be taken away, perhaps leaving the non-profit with massive budget and staff cuts. El Centro must develop internal leaders that will be able to take future leadership roles in various other fields and institutions. It is imperative for non-profits to nurture and develop future leaders, otherwise you end up with a void of younger leaders.

MALDEF has the opportunity to continually hire top-notch attorneys and to develop internships for future attorneys. MAOF also has the opportunity to externalize its marketing and public relations and to strengthen its grass roots.

Non-profits should seize upon the opportunity that major foundations are now willing to give multi-year grants in the range of $100,000 or more. The California Endowment, Eisner Foundation, and The California Wellness Foundation have approved multi-year grants for El Centro. This is key to sustaining long-term programs and social services. MALDEF, MAOF, and El Centro must seek out and apply for these innovative grants.

We also need to develop relationships with corporations and business leaders who are willing to support effective, local non-profits such as El Centro. It is a challenge to convince businesses to invest in non-profits, but it also is to their benefit to build good will and communication by doing so. Since we have the longevity, name recognition, and good reputation in Pasadena, we should be able to diversify fundraising in Pasadena and the San Gabriel Valley area. But it is always a work in progress. A good example of business leader who gives back to the community is Abel Ramirez, who is the owner of El Portal Restaurant in Pasadena.

Abel Ramirez came to the United States with hopes and dreams from Yucatan, Mexico. He now has turned those dreams into reality here in Pasadena. He is the current owner of El Portal Restaurant, Yahaira's Café, and The Coffee Tree. He has persevered through hard work and dedication.

Abel was born in Tekax, Yucatan. In 1963, he came to spend a summer vacation at his sister's house, but that summer stay was extended. He began working at the Huntington Hotel washing dishes, and quickly was promoted to various administrative positions. His tenure at the Huntington Hotel lasted over 15 years.

Abel was hired to manage Caltech's Athenaeum, and stayed as the General Manager for 17 years, sharing his skills related to Club operations. After running the Club, early in 1995 the idea to take over El Portal Restaurant was born. Abel opened El Portal, focusing on cuisine from his native Yucatan. His wife Rosalia has always been by his side, providing strength, motivation, and training the chefs to adopt authentic flavors of Yucatan.

Abel is a former Board member of Hillsides Home for Children. He is a founder and current board member for the Playhouse District Association. He is a current Board Member of the Pasadena Playhouse, and also serves on the Board of Foothill Vocational Services. Abel has been involved with the Tournament of Roses for over 28 years and is now a board member for the Pasadena Senior Center.

Abel has been married to Rosalia for over 40 years. He represents the hopes and aspirations of millions of immigrants who have come to the United States, and has contributed immensely to the Pasadena community. His love for children and senior citizens is evident through his actions. Abel is an inspirational leader and successful business owner who has never forgotten where he came from, and is proud of his roots. Abel has created and provided many, many jobs for people who need work and appreciate being given an opportunity to succeed through hard work. Non-profits are similar to actual businesses, what makes or breaks any organization is whether the employees are content there and are treated with dignity and respect.

Unfortunately, the threats in the internal environment of any non-profit are unmotivated and selfish sloth employees. Non-profits must hire employees who care about social issues and helping people. Complacency or fear of change can also cripple a non-profit. Other internal threats are negative board members and disloyal staff members. Internal leaks can be destructive — especially when an institution has a disgruntled and vindictive employee who wants to take revenge by any means necessary.

Threats in the external environment are many: a continual bad economy, corporations declaring bankruptcy, new non-profits offering the same services, negative relations with key elected officials, and a decrease in donor donations. Let's examine a specific case study of a huge corporation that is slowly going out of business, Blockbuster video stores. This example highlights how a Board of Directors can make or break a CEO. Also, Blockbuster offers a solid case study regarding the role of a Board of Directors.

The *Harvard Business Review* article "Blockbuster's Former CEO on Sparring with an Activist Shareholder" by John Antioco describes the challenges he faced as Chief Executive Officer (CEO) at Blockbuster.

Antioco resented the fact that Carl Icahn, well-known investor, decided in 2005 to buy 10 million shares of stock in Blockbuster to gain control of the corporation. "Expectations of failure were hovering over the company even before I joined in 1997. Most outsiders were convinced that our bricks-and-mortar video retail business would be killed off by market shifts and technological advances," wrote Antioco (Antioco, 2011, p. 39). The primary hypothesis is that Icahn's personal investment interests and greed and selfishness led to the downfall of Blockbuster.

What made Antioco's life hell was Carl Icahn's aggressive and micromanaging tactics in controlling Blockbuster, and his willingness to include two additional Board Members that would do his bidding and support his ideas, not Antioco's. When Boards decide to take control of an institution and undermine the CEO, many times these tactics backfire. However, it is a well-known fact that Boards usually get rid of CEO's who are not succeeding or are not bringing in enough profits. The corporate world can be heartless and cruel since making monetary profits is what mainly drives corporations. Some corporations even lose a sense of humanity by merely seeing its workforce as machines and tools to make money.

Antioco further writes that "when Directors with preconceived notions are determined to serve as obstacles to management's plans, it's hard to find a formula for *success*. Three years after my departure as CEO, Blockbuster declared bankruptcy" (Antioco, 2011, p. 40). Antioco had extensive experience in turning around businesses that were failing and making them into successful and profitable entities. He had management and leadership experience obtained through 20 years as a top manager at 7-Eleven; he was CEO at Circle K, and PepsiCo hired him as CEO of Taco Bell. Antioco proved to be an effective leader there because he listened to the senior managers and they implemented a new strategy that helped to make Taco Bell a powerhouse in the fast-food industry.

Antioco tells his readers that you have to listen to your staff and protect them when you are a CEO. Carl Icahn's role and experience in life was being an "activist shareholder" which means that he buys thousands of shares in different corporations and then pulls out his investment to make monumental profits. He could care less if people were laid off or fired in order to save costs. What he really cared about was making money, and he managed to undermine Antioco's leadership. Icahn wanted Antioco to resign, along with other Board Members. Unfortunately, many Board Members merely see companies as cash machines for themselves or for the stock holders.

Changes in technology and the introduction of the DVD did nothing to help Blockbuster remain competitive. Netflix was ahead of the curve by providing movies by mail. Antioco was trying to keep Blockbuster financially stable, by eliminating late fees of video rentals. "Those moves put Blockbuster back into growth mode" (Antioco, 2011, p. 41). This was a wonderful idea but Icahn and most of the Board of Directors did not agree with the elimination of late fees. This created further tensions. Especially when Antioco wanted to "spend $200 million to launch Blockbuster Online and another $200 million to eliminate late fees" (Antioco, 2011, p. 42).

These two moves really angered Icahn and he began writing letters to the shareholders to make Antioco look bad and to obtain full control of the company.

"Carl Icahn and his two chosen Directors were now on our Board of eight. Even though he lacked a majority, sheer force of will gave him a lot of power. Since it could be a formidable task, after a while the other Directors were disinclined to pick a fight with him. So within a few months he effectively controlled the Board" (Antioco, 2011, p. 42).

Antioco describes how Icahn did not follow protocol in the board meetings. He spoke his mind and interrupted anyone whenever he wanted. "Having contentious Directors was a nightmare; as management, we spent much of our time justifying everything we did" (Antioco, 2011, p. 43). Since Icahn now fully controlled the Blockbuster Board, he would question everything and opposed a lot of the ideas from management, along with the board members that he had recruited to back him up.

Antioco was also partially to blame, since he already received a monumental salary in the tens of millions. Plus he wanted to obtain a lofty bonus through executive compensation. The Board refused. This was the issue that broke the camel's back. Antioco negotiated to leave the company and he stated "we finally agreed that I'd leave the company in July 2007 and would be paid a negotiated bonus plus an exit package. The board environment had become very frustrating and stressful, but instead of resigning and walking away with nothing, I had cut a deal giving me a major portion of the pay I was entitled to" (Harvard Business Review, p. 43).

The Board did choose a new CEO named Jim Keyes to run Blockbuster. He had great retail experience, but he did not have the technology marketing experience to help Blockbuster survive the changing times. On September 23, 2010 Blockbuster filed for bankruptcy.

Eventually Antioco cashed out the stocks he had in Blockbuster and invested them in Netflix.

Many lessons can be deduced from this case study. Antioco was driven by greed and promoted hedge funds. He knew how to pressure corporations to make profits, increasing the value of shares. The ultimate lesson here is that profits are what drive investors like Icahn, and CEOs like Antioco are compensated heftily, while the employees make minimum wage and often are kept as part timers, to avoid providing health care coverage to them.

It is a tragedy that Blockbuster stores are going out of business due to the mismanagement of people like Icahn. Now thousands of people are unemployed, and we no longer can continue the tradition of going to Blockbuster videos to rent our favorite movies, to see by ourselves or with our families.

Boards of Directors can definitely make major mistakes and CEO's are ultimately the ones to blame since it is easy for a group of people who are given governance powers to blame one individual. Antioco is definitely courageous by writing this article in the Harvard Business Review. I applaud his honesty and courage in telling some of the truth of what led to Blockbuster's fall. Some corporations have fallen due to the personal interests of boards of directors in making profits for themselves. The cable television program *American Greed* often profiles individuals driven by insatiable greed and usually destroy a corporation since they choose to engage in fraud and corruption.

Some of the key threats against non-profits are internal dissension by staff and board members not supporting the Executive Director, similar to the case of Blockbuster's Board of Directors. Boards should and do remove Executive Directors or CEO's who do, in fact, engage in illegal, fraudulent, and corrupt activities. Another threat is the issue of leaked information, whether from a non-profit, the Pentagon, or a major corporation. Therefore, Executive

Directors of non-profits must be highly aware of external and internal threats. Cyber spying and stealing of information via technology is a major threat for non-profits too.

Another issue affecting non-profits is bullying. It not only takes place in our public schools or among young people, but in many workplaces. And it can lead to the destruction of any institution if bullies are allowed to thrive without consequences. We must do everything in our power to counter bullies, especially in the non-profit world. Bullying must not be tolerated.

Pop stars Eminem and Lady Gaga recently admitted that they were victims of bullying, and we applaud them for making this a relevant issue that should not just apply to youth, but to adults too. It is primarily the adults who set examples with regard to bullying, and it is imperative to include the word "civility" in our national discourse. If you ask high school and college students, would they know what *civility* even means? One broad definition would be treating others with dignity and respect. Let us explore this elementary concept further, via a book analysis, since we have simply forgotten what civility is all about.

Civility: Manners, Morals, and the Etiquette of Democracy by Stephen L. Carter is a thought provoking book that focuses on why we have lost good manners and respect towards others, and what we need to do to recapture *civility* in our society.

Carter focuses on historical examples and real-life scenarios that illustrate how the United States has evolved from being a young Democracy to one with utter disregard for mutual respect. The author provides ideas on how we can recapture civility, by focusing on our personal actions and treating others with dignity and respect. The key is to stop the vicious cycle of incivility and bullying by not condoning or participating in it.

Stephen L. Carter chose to write about civility, since he has personally witnessed the drastic decline of respectful treatment in U.S. society. He uses personal experience as well as history to make this point. He proves his point by reviewing political debates, campaigns, and the role television plays in denigrating and destroying the reputation of opponents.

The book calls for civility and respect towards others, even when they are rude to us. Of course, it is easier said than done. But we must continually strive to be the opposite of negative, disrespectful, and uncivil role models or bosses. At times, naturally, we all fall short in practice. Carter's ultimate goal is for us to grasp what civility means, and treat others with respect and tolerance. Because civility is a topic often forgotten, ignored, and misunderstood, Carter's book is still relevant and valuable, even though it is over a decade old.

Where I disagree with him is in his statements that religions have not created or expressed incivility. In some cases, opposing religious views have created tensions and even violence. He misses an opportunity to mention the

European One Hundred Year War between Protestants and Catholics and the continual conflict between Palestine and Israel.

Overall, it is a good book, but it does lack in some areas. This book talks indirectly about how social inequities have led us to become a nation of intolerance and mistreatment. . It does not help explain how we have evolved to become an intolerant nation. However, the truth of the matter is that this nation was established with principles of intolerance, and the author only touches lightly on this topic. He could have gone more in depth to further explore the topic of social, political, and economic inequities that have fed fuel to incivility.

Fortunately, Carter does talk about slavery and how the owners of slaves may have practiced "civility" in their political and economic interactions, but the truth is that in the late 1700s, the United States adopted unjust and inhumane attitudes that African Americans, Native Americans, and other minorities were inherently inferior. Yes, the U.S. Constitution afforded us many rights, which we continue to cherish and value. But it took a Civil War to end slavery, and centuries more for women, African Americans, and other minorities to be treated with dignity and respect. The U.S. Constitution had to ultimately be amended to allow African Americans and women the right to vote.

The author successfully points out that the Catholic Church and other religious institutions have tried to influence television networks to focus on civility in their programming content and visuals. But because the television industry is driven by viewer ratings and paid advertising, we know that it will continue to feature topics and images that perpetuate incivility through the obsessive promotion of violence.

This book has now taken on added relevance, as everyone is now looking to blame others for our social ills during the economic crisis. Ultimately, bullying must not be tolerated in our households, school, workplace, and especially in the non-profit world, or among activists who sometimes may feel that they stand on higher moral ground. We must treat even our adversaries with dignity and respect; otherwise we will set a bad example for our future young leaders and activists.

We have seen a rise in violent shootings throughout the United States. We also see campaigns purposely using dirty and uncivil tactics to destroy the character of political candidates. This book must have great potential to improve our daily dialogue with others, promoting better communication and respect for all.

And yes, the workplace and schools must adopt policies of zero tolerance towards incivility and bullying. The leaders of non-profits must set an example that bullying is not acceptable and leadership has a trickle-down effect. If you have a police chief, mayor or superintendent that is a bully, then the rank and file, mid-level management, and other employees may begin to even tolerate or copy this behavior.

Non-profit leaders must be strong and competent. Otherwise their groups may suffer bad staff recruitment, inadequate delivery of programs, and poor fundraising efforts. Incompetent leadership can actually lead a non-profit to cutting staff, closing programs, or losing critical funding that may force a non-profit to close its doors permanently.

Non-profits should also consider collaborating and even applying for joint funding, while steering clear of competing with and badmouthing each other. Foundations do in fact check around on the reputation of a non-profit's executive director and board members.

Jack Shakely, who is president emeritus of the California Community Foundation, stated in an op-ed published by the L.A. Times that, "It is really hard to judge the merits of most nonprofit organizations programmatically. Are people smarter, healthier, do they drive better, get fewer divorces or smoke less as a direct result of a nonprofit organization's intervention? These are the questions we should be asking, and there are many who are trying to do just that every day, internally in nonprofits, and in universities and research centers across the country" (Shakely, 2012).

Recruiting highly professional Board Members can bring substance to a non-profit organization. New board members can contribute oxygen and new ideas, but their number-one priority should be to help with fundraising. Many foundations require that board members give or get donations. This helps to empower a non-profit, and sets a good example.

El Centro's greatest strategic strength is its legacy, name recognition, solid reputation that goes deep into the fabric of Pasadena, and the fact that it has the key contacts at all the major institutions in Pasadena. It knows how to fundraise and also does a great job in getting the word out via the media. It has developed a strong name in the Pasadena area. El Centro already has a solid track record of applying for grants and completing them effectively, and a reputation as a good steward of funding from foundations, corporations, and the government. The weaknesses of key competitors stem from their short track record in Pasadena and the San Gabriel Valley.

El Centro de Accion Social has the potential to become one of the largest and most well-known non-profits in the San Gabriel Valley — not just Pasadena — by helping the low-income community through youth and senior citizen programs. This will give El Centro a fundraising base that spans a broader geographic area, and an opportunity to seek larger long-term grants from foundations and the federal government. Hopefully, El Centro will become financially stable and independent.

Its niche is serving the low-income Latino community in Pasadena and San Gabriel Valley area. El Centro de Accion Social in Pasadena is pretty much it, with regard to helping youth and senior citizens with day-to-day programs and social services. I am not minimizing or purposely ignoring other non-profits that do in fact help Latinos, they are many, and much credit should be given to them. But what's unique about El Centro is that it was founded by Latino activists and is led and run by Latinos and Latinas. This, in turn, sets a great example to our youth that we serve — it tells them that we have the skills, intelligence, and capacity to run major non-profits, corporations, and institutions. Many times, due to discrimination, minority led non-profits are not funded by Foundations at the same level as mainstream non-profits. Also, a certain aura of distrust does exist when it is a minority-led non-profit, especially since many times these non-profits are targeted by law enforcement and put under surveillance, since they are perceived to be a threat to society, provide advocacy, and have major influence in mobilizing community members to denounce injustices. J. Edgar Hoover was known to target the NAACP and the Black Panther movement. These groups were constantly monitored and infiltrated by government agents. Many times they provided key information to police departments who did, in fact, targeted and purposely murdered Black Panther leaders. We hope that they illegal tactics are no longer being implemented that target law abiding activists.

Fortunately, El Centro has balanced its budget in each of the last eight years. We do have small reserves that allow us to apply for, and obtain, key funding and resources. El Centro may become larger, but it must not forget the reason it exists: to represent and help the voiceless and faceless.

El Centro stands for social justice and seeks to improve the lives of youth and senior citizens in a tangible manner. The core beliefs are to help the poor and empower others through advocacy for those who cannot speak for themselves or are afraid to do so.

The critical success factors will be: consistent and effective fundraising, creating and offering top-notch programs, hiring competent staff members who have big hearts to help others, recruiting professional and committed Board Members, and ultimately obtaining support from more foundations, corporations, and secure government grants. The strategic thrust will be to raise enough funds to hire a development director in order to continue to raise funds, maintain key staff, recruit new board members, and develop and implement an up-to-date strategic plan that serves as a roadmap for the future. The road to success is having a competent and motivated Executive Director implement long-term goals and implement our mission.

The operating goals are to raise $500,000 on a yearly basis. The ideal plan is to evolve into a $1 to $2 million institution that will be known throughout the San Gabriel Valley — from Glendale, Monrovia, Duarte, Azusa and Whittier to Pomona.

Ultimately, low-income community members will benefit most if El Centro, MALDEF, and MAOF remain financially stable. Society as a whole benefits through the effective and responsible work of non-profits. Yes, we are all in this together, the poor, the middle class, and the rich. We all need each other. The rich need the poor and middle class to buy their products, and the rich need to see that investing and donating to non-profits is critical, and will ultimately benefit their bottom line — profits. Wells Fargo Foundation conducted a study that did, in fact, indicate that businesses that donate to non-profits develop good community will, resulting in more profits and satisfied customers. For example, State Farm, Union Bank, Kaiser Permanente, Southern California Edison, and other foundations and corporations are key supporters of El Centro. This collaboration and support helps our economy and creates jobs, while non-profits remain the safety valve that reduces the risk of social upheaval.

El Centro de Accion Social will continue to be the voice of the faceless of the San Gabriel Valley.

Chapter Six

How to Organize Fundraisers

People will make fun of you and criticize, but will not help you to implement a fundraiser or obtain foundation grants. Many will not even be willing to introduce you to potential donors or funders. Many others will want you to fail as an activist. When you decide to plan and implement an annual fundraiser, you will be questioned and ridiculed for wanting to change the culture of the organization. Remaining a grassroots organization, living on a lean budget and not having enough resources to make payroll is ineffective non-profit leadership. When you decide to do an annual fundraiser, you must take the bull by the horns and make it happen. Here are the tools. When you believe in something you have to make it happen. Convince your Board of Directors that it is possible. Get majority or unanimous support.

First, find an affordable location, at a nice, professional venue. Not Motel 6. Find a classy and prestigious local hotel where you can have a sit-down dinner. Meet with the hotel representative to go over prices of the meal and overall costs of the event. Set a date and time for the event, and then secure the location. Simultaneously you have to find a great master of ceremonies, awesome keynote speaker, and then decide who to honor. You have to juggle identifying and getting commitments from all of these key people. One of the toughest things will be to establish a date and time for the event, since important people are often travelling and usually busy. But it is possible to pull it off. You have to believe in yourself and God.

Then, you have to organize an honorary dinner committee, set meeting dates, secure sponsorships, prepare formal invitations, mail them out, make phone calls, recruit volunteers to help you, and keep the Board involved and informed. Ideally, recruit two Board Members to be dinner co-chairs. Also, find someone who will prepare a video to be shown at the event and also select key music.

Maintain civility by not allowing people to get too drunk and disorderly. Do not allow gate-crashers who do not pay to just show up and leech off your event. Besides getting in free, they could also take your contacts for their personal agendas or self-interest. You and your staff, Board, and volunteers have worked too hard for that. The purpose of an annual fundraiser is to raise money. Bottomline. It is excellent to recognize amazing honorees but the reality is that you need to raise funds to continue the programs of the organization.

You also have to find nice table flowers and professional awards (plaques), and you have to make sure that the sound system and video system work beforehand. Also, make sure that the MC keeps the event focused and on schedule. Make sure that the food is well-prepared and appropriate for all guests. Making seat arrangements is quite an art, and be sure you prepare a sign-in system, and recruit student volunteers who will welcome and guide guests to their tables. Young people always feel proud to be part of a major annual event. Ask one or two of the young people to say a few words at the event. We need to hear that the organization has helped improve the lives of the people being served.

Also, it is not a bad idea to have a religious leader to say a prayer.

A panel discussion took place to discuss the 20th Anniversary of the Los Angeles Riots/Uprising. Panelists included: Randy Jurado Ertll, executive director of El Centro de Accion Social, Inc.; Dr. Maulana Karenga, Professor and Chair - Department of Africana Studies at California State University, Long Beach; Do Hyung Kim, Attorney at Law & active community leader; Rev. Eric P. Lee, President and CEO of the Southern Christian Leadership Conference - Los Angeles (SCLC).

Don Smith, Lifelong Religious Activist and Alumnus of Occidental College.

David Allgood, Environmental Activist and Political Director of the California League of Conservation Voters (CLCV).

Manny Contreras, Lifelong Activist and President of the Pasadena Mexican-American History Association.

Tecumseh Shackelford, Founder and Leader of the Mentoring and Partnership for Youth Development Program at John Muir High School.

Jaylene Moseley, Philanthropist, Activist, and Leader of the Flintridge Center in Pasadena, CA.

Martin Castro, current President and Chief Executive Officer of the Mexican American Opportunity Foundation (MAOF). Mr. Castro oversees a MAOF budget of over $60 million and he is a lifelong community advocate and effective non profit leader.

Karen Lee, Activist and Board Member of the Pasadena Presbyterian Church.

Dr. Terrence Roberts and Renatta Cooper, President of the School Board of Education for Pasadena Unified School District & Lifelong Activist. Renatta continues the Civil Rights legacy of Dr. Roberts.

Lorna Holt, Student Activist from Cornell University and Professional Engineer.

Jorge Nuno, founder of the Nuevo South nonprofit organization in South L.A. and successful Business Owner.

Chapter Seven

How to Organize and Mobilize Community Members

Organizing, motivating, and mobilizing community members is one of the hardest jobs in the world — especially if you are trying to mobilize the poor. Many have to work two or three jobs, earn minimum wages, have no health insurance, have children to raise, and can barely afford to pay the rent or mortgage. They have many internal family challenges. Hence when an activist comes along trying to mobilize them, they are rightfully suspicious. There are exceptions, but most activists come and go, and rarely live or stay in a particular community.

Activists, by nature, are mobile, and always looking for the next exciting issue. They often get bored with the same people and same issues. For the most part, they have innate energy, curiosity, and restlessness. Social movements must strive to be representative of the diverse fabric of the United States. Let's look at the Occupy Movement, for an example of a group that did not succeed at recruiting minorities. Some will deny this fact, since they will say I had "one" African American, Latino, or Asian friend who were part of it.

Predominantly white low-income and middle-class individuals joined the Occupy Movement to denounce corporate greed. Feeling frustrated by the inequities in our economic system, activists led months of protests throughout the United States. The Occupy Movement needed to recruit minorities, not only to accurately reflect the ethnic diversity of the country, but to make the point that economic injustice falls most heavily on the backs of minorities.

The median wealth of white households is 20 times that of black households and 18 times that of Hispanic households, according to the Pew Research Center.

For their part, Latinos, African-Americans and other minorities would have benefited from joining the Occupy Movement in massive numbers. But they did not, and a great opportunity was missed — especially for minority youth — who could have learned by participating in a nonviolent social justice struggle.

Minorities needed to feel welcome and they didn't. But the truth is that White Americans and minorities are all in this together. The U.S. Census recently released statistics that designate half of the U.S. population, 146 million, as poor or low income.

The Occupy movement did a great job shedding light on the economic disparities in our country. But it needed to find common cause with the labor, civil-rights, and immigrant-rights movements, both to broaden its base, and to build the kind of political force that can make our economy more just for everybody.

To sustain a long-term social justice movement that fights for economic and social fairness, the leadership should not overlook minorities. But the leadership of the Occupy Movement was mostly discouraged, and many members were beaten and arrested by the police. Many became disillusioned and quit.

However, an activist must learn to make long-term commitments and not just use community members by mobilizing them, getting their hopes up, and then leaving them high and dry. Many Executive Directors and activists are looking for their next jobs, too. To make an impact an activist must put in at least ten years with a specific community and issue. An activist must get to know other community activists and leaders, and it takes a while to establish communication, trust, loyalty, and a strong following. Also, voter registration efforts and campaigns are good, but more is needed to fully empower people. Organizing must be done in baby steps. Just because people are registered to vote, doesn't mean that they will, or that they will take the time to inform themselves about the issues. Voter registration feels good — but we have to go beyond feeling good and getting people to the polls. We must actually train future leaders who will run for public office and can make changes for the greater good. As our former President Bill Clinton likes to say, "We are all in this together." And I say *hell yes we are!*

Candidates from any political party, especially Republicans and Democrats, must strive to gain the Latino and African-American vote — not by pandering, but by looking after the needs of these two groups. Many of these are shared, such as stopping foreclosures, providing decent jobs, improving graduation rates, and steering youth away from gangs and prisons.

Latinos, as a community, do have their own distinct needs, as well, and candidates need to address these, including immigration reform and bilingual education.

But the bread-and-butter issues that affect Latinos and African-Americans also resonate with low-income and moderate-income whites. After all, most voters simply seek to have affordable housing, secure jobs, health insurance, enough money to feed and educate their children, and Social Security and Medicare benefits for retirement. These are universal concerns.

Let us vote for the candidates who are most committed to serving the needs of our multicultural society, those who can reunite and revitalize our country through action, not just promises. The future of our country is at stake and activists are in the frontlines. And yes, social movements are much more effective when they include ethnic diversity.

Once an activist decides to stick around, he or she then has to get to know people. Personal visits to individual homes are one way. Voter registration is not enough. Taking over public spaces and parks is not enough. Especially since city governments have the authority to evict and arrest protesters. Also, an activist has to be willing to have many breakfast, lunch, or dinner meetings, which are essential and can get expensive. Fortunately, sometimes just having water or coffee will suffice. Activists must not just seek out elected officials or the elite, they also must meet with the poor single parent, individuals who live in the projects, and other disenfranchised community members. The activist must learn how to see and treat a homeless person with dignity and respect. We are no better than that homeless person in the streets or park — except that we may have had more privileges and opportunities in life.

An activist must find out the needs of the community through direct conversations, or by conducting a door-to-door survey. Once the issues are clearly identified, the activist can establish community meetings or forums and have open discussions. Then if necessary, community members can decide whether they want to mobilize and petition City Hall or the school district board. The activist cannot dictate, tell the community members how to think, or just bark orders. Nor can we tolerate would-be cult leaders like the infamous Jim Jones, of the People's Temple, who served people from the Oakland and San Francisco areas of California. He led thousands of people to Guyana, South America, where eventually demanded that they drink poison and commit massive suicide. Some parents were so brainwashed that they even murdered their own children.

So while an activist must sometimes play psychologist, social worker, and even spiritual leader, he or she must not become a cult leader or a manipulator. Followers need to beware of demagogues, or activists that like to mislead people and create great conflict and tensions. Leaders must lead by example, and they must stick around when it gets hot in the kitchen. An activist cannot be weak-hearted or wimpy. You must have the courage to confront those in power, and be ready when they decide to come after you. Especially with the paranoia that the September 11th attacks created throughout the United States. Now people who are of Middle Eastern decent are profiled and perceived to be a threat to U.S. national security.

Once you mobilize the community, you have to have specific goals to achieve. If those small battles or issues are won, then credit must be given to everyone, even to observers who didn't do much, but will be able to share the stories of how the community finally decided to mobilize. Once a victory occurs, bystanders and even critics begin to take credit too.

It will be one battle after another. If you are successful, much responsibility will come to you, and there will be no turning back. You will want to make social change to the point where you cannot sleep, thinking of all the issues and social injustices that need to be tackled and made right. Just remember what Maya Angelou eloquently stated "To those who are given much, much is expected."

Be a transparent leader. Avoid using community members to do your work or engaging in gossip or rumors. The job of the activist is to resolve social issues and to help improve the lives of poor community members who most of the time do not have anyone defending them.

Yes, it is exhausting, but you have been forewarned. Resources are usually so scarce that everyone will want that little piece of cake you may have gained through much sweat and tears. Some social movements shed blood. Some followers of Martin Luther King, Jr., Cesar Chavez and Nelson Mandela were murdered.

Rejections, insults, and failures will often occur along the way. It is not enough to get beaten by the police, and it is not a good idea to seek out a beating. But it may happen anyway, especially if you are a frontline, no-holds-barred activist. You may become a target of law enforcement, especially if you are denouncing police brutality. But then again, you may just only be asking for positive changes to take place within law enforcement. Sometimes you have to serve as a diplomat and peacemaker among different interest groups and factions. You will sometimes have to become an expert in crafting policy in order to make fundamental changes. In reality — according to a report released by the Police Assessment Resource Center, (PARC), which focused on the Los Angeles County Sheriff's Department — policies governing the use of lethal force by police departments need revision. This is an issue that greatly impacts Latinos and African Americans.

This is sadly illustrated by the fatal shooting of Kendrec McDade, 19, of Azusa. Such a tragedy may seem out of place in a nice city like Pasadena, but McDade was shot there on March 24, 2012 after he allegedly reached into his waistband while running from police near the intersection of Orange Grove Boulevard and Sunset Avenue. What is the most ironic and tragic fact is that Kendrec was a member of Pasadena Police Department's Police Activities League (PAL) youth program. But because of the color of his skin, he was most likely profiled and perceived as a threat.

The PARC semiannual report, compiled by Special Counsel Merrick J. Bobb, states that investigators "focus in particular on 'state-of-mind' or 'perception' shootings where deputies perceive, accurately or not, that a suspect may be armed or going for a gun. We are concerned to see that state-of-mind shootings rose by more than 50 percent in the past year. We note that 2010 had the highest proportion of hit shootings in recent years in which the suspect was unarmed. This fact was further reflected in 2010 in the number of 'waistband shootings' where the suspect was shot at upon reportedly reaching for his waistband" (Bobb, 2012).

The report further states, "61 percent of suspects in state-of-mind shootings turn out to be unarmed. What troubles us is that African American or Latino youth are more likely to be the subject of a mistaken perception of dangerousness than is a white or Asian person."

The report goes on to state that "Latinos appear to be significantly overrepresented in shooting incidents in comparison to their overall arrest rates, while white suspects are underrepresented."

Regardless of race or ethnicity, police-related beatings and shootings need to be investigated and monitored more closely. Let us not forget the July 5, 2012 fatal beating of Kelly Thomas, a homeless schizophrenic, by Fullerton police officers Jay Cicinelli and Manuel Ramos.

We must remind law enforcement officials to act in a way that creates safety and trust, not just in affluent areas, but also in poor and middle-class neighborhoods. What occurred in Fullerton was a tragedy and an injustice. But Kelly Thomas' case might have been ignored, if he had not been the son of Ron Thomas, a retired Orange County sheriff's deputy. Ron Thomas led a citywide effort to bring justice to his murdered son. He was persistent and not afraid, especially because he had countless supporters and knew how our legal system favors the more affluent.

Wealthy individuals and powerful bureaucracies can hire high-caliber criminal defense attorneys, while the poor usually get convicted and sentenced since they cannot afford seasoned, well-known, expensive lawyers. Fortunately, we do have advocacy groups such as the American Civil Liberties Union (ACLU) who remain a watchdog in relation to many social and legal issues. What is admirable about the ACLU is that it receives no government funding and therefore is free to criticize government policies, practices, and actions. Kris Ockershauser, has served as the President of the ACLU Pasadena/Foothills chapter and she is actively involved in very important social justice issues, including issues related to police abuse and youth rights. She usually tackles issues that many are afraid to discuss openly since many community members are afraid to speak up. Therefore, the ACLU continues to play an invaluable role in our society, especially in relation to issues of police abuse.

Officers in police departments around the country have used lethal force in many questionable circumstances. Here are some of the most notorious in the last couple of decades — at least those that the public is aware of. Many cases go unnoticed or unreported because the families of the victims are afraid to speak up or do not know how to access media attention and political support.

Back in 1991, a Salvadoran immigrant was shot by an African-American police officer and rioting occurred for two days in the Mount Pleasant area in Washington D.C. Lack of bilingual police officers and cultural insensitivity resulted in distrust and antagonism between the community and the police department.

Of course, we cannot forget the savage beating of Rodney King by four white LAPD police officers. These officers were acquitted on April 29, 1992, and the community was so outraged that rioting lasted for six days, resulting in many deaths and more than $1 billion in property damages.

On Jan. 1, 2009, a white transit officer in Oakland shot and killed Oscar Grant, a black man, while he was being subdued on the ground.

City Councils, police oversight commissions, and independent community panels must devise clearer and more stringent policies for the use of lethal force. Let's just hope and pray that these types of shootings can be prevented in the future, through use of better tactics to subdue or disarm individuals who pose a clear and present danger to civilians and police officers. Also, police officers should also be trained in how to better communicate with and treat individuals who have mental disorders and/or physical challenges.

The Police Assessment Resource Center says that "the problems we describe can be resolved or substantially ameliorated by further training, strict accountability, and focused attention." If that doesn't happen, distrust of police will only continue to rise, not just in poor communities, but in middle-class areas as well. That's the last thing we need.

As an activist, you may become an ally of police departments, and/or be asked to serve on police panels, commissions, or boards, whose goals are to improve relations between law enforcement and minority communities.

Also, with time and maturity, an activist may turn to social networks, blogging, or writing. Of course, once in a while I will go back to my community organizing roots and put on my activist hat. I don't have a cape yet.

In a nutshell, you can mobilize and motivate people, but putting an organizing plan in place will provide tangible results. Do not over-promise, or pretend to be some sort of hero or messiah. Sometimes you will have to negotiate with your antagonists, and they may eventually become your allies. But then again, sometimes your allies may turn on you. So you never know what can happen through activism and community organizing. Some social movements have been ruined and tarnished due to internal differences and infighting among the leadership.

Chapter Eight

How to Deal with Boards of Directors and Bureaucracies

One of an activist's biggest challenges is to deal with the Board of Directors, since technically they are the macro policy body that is responsible for governance. Your boss is not an individual, but a group of people who are responsible to oversee the finances and work that the activist or executive director is doing.

If you are doing a good job, the Board will be very supportive. But once you start to slip up, the Board may pressure you or talk about replacing you. Of course, you may be too busy organizing, mobilizing, and fundraising to realize that the Board is not happy. Then the board meeting comes and one of the Board members may ask for your resignation. Not a good day.

As an effective activist or leader, you must keep your Board informed via e-mail, phone, or regularly scheduled Directors meetings. You have to become an expert in financing and budget. You cannot and must not overspend whatever is in the annual operating budget. If you overspend, you will end up in a deficit. You have to do everything in your power to fundraise and to maintain a balanced budget. Once you prove that you are an effective administrator or manager, the board may have more trust in your abilities and become more supportive. The key is for the Executive Director and Board President to have good communication and trust.

You also must deal with bureaucracies such as city government, school districts, police departments, fire departments, universities, and other institutions. They will each have a specific role or interest within your non-profit. Many times community members or politicians will threaten Executive Directors by demanding or requesting meetings with individual Board Members or request meetings with the full board. Many times these are intimidation tactics and executive directors who are doing things right should not allow for such bullying, intimidation, or blackmailing tactics. Sometimes these unethical threats need to be documented and exposed.

The key is to develop relationships and coalitions. But as an activist, sooner or later you will get into hot water with a bureaucracy. For example, if police brutality takes place in your community, you cannot remain quiet. If you do, then you are complacent, and not doing a good job of representing the needs of the community. Slowly but surely, the chief, mayor, or city manager may get upset that "the activist" began to ask questions and make trouble, especially if the media gets involved. The activist may end up on the front page of the local newspaper criticizing the city or school district. This won't make city leaders happy, since they usually like to hear good news. But we will be creating a much more effective and socially conscious society if we work together to fix the inequities and injustices.

Chapter Nine

Concepts of Community Organizing and Coalition Building

Poor people are invisible, especially African Americans and Latinos who live in the poor ghettos of America. This is not new; it has existed for decades. I grew up in South Central and saw the injustices of poverty, poor housing, inadequate and unsafe school facilities and police brutality first hand. Community organizing and coalition building in poor communities is truly a tough job — but someone has to do it.

Fortunately, now African Americans and Latinos do play a key role in being the swing vote, and can no longer be taken for granted or ignored. It is becoming almost impossible to win the Presidency with only the white vote. In the past, we've heard enough hollow promises, while young African American and Latino children keep joining gangs, dropping out of school and killing each other. The pattern of unequal distribution of wealth can be seen throughout poor communities, where resources are scarce. A few churches do provide hope and guidance for many families, but city government also needs to provide more opportunities. Poor people pay taxes too. Karen Lee, who is Chinese American, serves on the Board of Trustees for the Pasadena Presbyterian Church. She attended and graduated from Occidental College and obtained her Master's degree from University of Kansas in public administration. She now gives back to the community by serving on the Board of the Presbyterian Church. She cares about helping youth and also the homeless. She says that through the technical definition of homelessness, she was homeless for six months. Therefore, she knows how it is to struggle and suffer. Now she is actively involved in various social justice issues.

After the reelection of President Barack Obama, the truth of the matter is that millions of low-income voters can make a difference in determining who will become our future Presidents. However, we have to continue to remind political candidates that they can no longer ignore or dismiss low-income voters.

Latinos and African Americans also must strive to build coalitions around issues that will benefit both ethnic groups. African-Americans and Latinos have too much in common not to get along better.

Both communities face high unemployment rates, high dropout rates, systemic poverty, gang violence, a disproportionate number of prison inmates, and continual discrimination.

So why do so many African-Americans resent Latin American immigrants, and why do so many Latinos fear African-Americans? The difficult issues that divide us include immigration, job competition, bilingual education and political representation. We need to address them a respectful and thoughtful manner.

Some African-American and Latino leaders have tried to form alliances. But this has proven more difficult than you might think.

Take the big immigrant rights marches over the past decade or so. The pro-immigrant Latino leadership did not do enough outreach to include a wide representation of African-American leaders and organizations. And few African-American leaders and community members participated in this movement.

We need to accentuate the history of alliances between African-Americans and Latinos. We should stress that Mexicans played an important role in the Underground Railroad during slavery. Creating a southern route, Mexicans enabled an estimated 10,000 escaped slaves to arrive in freedom south of the border. And we should also recall that Cesar Chavez was a kindred spirit with Martin Luther King Jr.

And we all should be sensitive about the words we choose and the claims we make. During massive pro-immigrant rights marches, some Latino leaders began to say that the immigrant rights movement was the new civil rights movement. This infuriated many African-Americans, who asked where all the Latinos were during the civil rights struggle, from which they later benefitted.

This unnecessary infighting and distrust must come to an end. Both communities have suffered tremendously, and neither side can deny it. We should come together to demand that gang violence be curtailed, dropout rates be reduced, jobs be created for both communities, and hate crimes be wiped out.

African-Americans and Latinos alike simply want to achieve the American dream: to have a decent education, a stable job with benefits, to be able to buy a house and a car, and to provide food, shelter and clothing to their children.

We should help each other achieve this dream. We cannot continue to blame each other, much less prey on each other. And we should not compete for the title of the country's most victimized minority group. That is a losing game. We must start by studying and respecting each other's history and culture, and then work together for a common cause. Cheryl Hubbard, is a former South Central resident who moved to Pasadena. She helped to create Mothers on the Move and she continues to be a staunched activist who advocates for peace and unity between African Americans and Latinos. She is African American and she personally met Cesar Chavez in the fields and she remembers that he was a quiet, humble man, but with a big heart and courage of a lion. He defended the rights of the poor.

The poor must demand more police protection, not police abuse, for their neighborhoods. African American and Latino youth must not be criminalized just because they live in poor neighborhoods with few opportunities. Congress and the president must work together to create viable opportunities, programs and jobs in the ghettos and barrios of America.

These voters also want their children to obtain a quality education. The youth who live in poor communities deserve to have more qualified and compassionate teachers. In the past, public schools with high poverty rates would usually get teachers who are fully credentialed or prepared to teach. Fortunately, now the under the Governor's office, the Commission on Teacher Credentialing (CTC) has raised the bar by increasing the requirements of becoming a fully credentialed public school teacher. We cannot set low expectations for our students or allow mediocre performance. We want them to be prepared and qualified to attend community colleges or any of the top universities in the nation.

We must offer our young people hope and make them realize that they cannot throw away their futures. Public school administrators, school board members, and public school union leaders have to come to the table and continue to negotiate fair teacher contracts. One of the toughest jobs is being a teacher. The parent and Principal demands are great, teaching responsibilities are tremendous, and expectations are extremely high. It is exhausting but it has to be done with a long lasting commitment and passion. After parents, teachers are a fundamental influence in the lives of children. Teachers practically serve as role models and many times are seen as super humans. But we have to provide more resources to parents, especially Latino and African American, to be become more actively involved in the education of their children. The public and private schools must make minority students and parents feel welcomed. In reality, many public schools remain open due to the high enrollment of minority students, and through average daily attendance (ADA). ADA funds keep these schools open, providing comfortable jobs for school administrators, principals, and teachers. Let us admit it: the retirement plans for public school employees are very good, especially if you compare them to retirement plans that non- profits may have. Some non-profits are financially struggling so much that they cannot even provide retirement plans. Talk about injustices. What can an activist do when they reach the age of 62 or above with no retirement plan? The sad reality is that many have to live on minimal social security benefits (if they qualify), and continually struggle to pay the rent, buy food, pay the bills, pay health insurance, fill the car tank with gasoline, and afford medication. Yes, just like teachers, activists are merely human, trying to economically survive, yet at the same time, make a positive difference in our society.

We have to continually remind low-income voters not to squander the opportunity to vote. They must value their power of their vote. Some activists were murdered during the Civil Rights movement, while they fought for voting rights. Let us not forget that people have died for us to have better opportunities. One outstanding Civil Rights leader I recently personally met is Dr. Terrence Roberts, one of the "Little Rock Nine," the students who helped to integrate public schools in Little Rock, Arkansas. Dr. Roberts is now part of the Little Rock Nine Foundation. Its web site states:

> Terrence J. Roberts was a 15 year old junior when he entered Little Rock Central High school. Despite the daily harassment, he completed his junior year, but moved with his family to Los Angeles the following year and graduated from Los Angeles High School in 1959. Dr. Roberts received a BA in sociology from California State University at Los Angeles in 1967. This was followed by an MS in Social Welfare in 1970 from the University of California at Los Angeles in 1970 and a Ph.D. in psychology from Southern Illinois University in 1976.
>
> Dr. Roberts is CEO of Terrence J. Roberts & Associates, a management consultant firm devoted to fair and equitable practices. A much sought after speaker and presenter, Dr. Roberts maintains a private psychology practice and lectures and presents workshops and seminars on a wide variety of topics.
>
> Dr. Roberts is the recipient of the Spingarn Medal and the Congressional Gold Medal. He serves on the boards of the Economic Resources Center in Southern California, the Western Justice Center Foundation, and the Little Rock Nine Foundation.
>
> Dr. Roberts and his wife Rita are the parents of two adult daughters and live in Pasadena, California (Little Rock Nine Foundation web site)

Terrence Roberts is an example of a young man who when he was just fifteen years old — faced immensely challenging circumstances, and chose to face fear head-on. He now contributes to society by writing books, providing powerful, deep, intellectual presentations and helping many people through his kind words and example of perseverance. He is an activist we can emulate and look up to as a positive role model.

Activists need to learn key concepts that can be implemented in a practical manner. I learned these from reading the community organizing teachings of Saul Alinsky. These were similar to the ones used by President Barack

Obama during his community organizing years in Chicago. Neither a Socialist nor a Muslim, Obama was indeed born in Hawaii.

Many organizers learned key concepts from Alinsky, including Cesar Chavez. Fred Rose Sr. worked closely with Alinski and eventually taught these same organizing skills to Chavez, who eventually became a regional and then national hero by establishing the United Farm Workers (UFW). Activists should be required to read about Saul Alinsky, lest we forget the legacy of many great activists.

Case in point, another great leader that time has forgotten is Ernesto Galarza. He obtained his undergraduate degree from Occidental College in Los Angeles and then a Master's in history from Stanford University in 1929. He later received a Ph.D. from Columbia University with honors in history. Galarza passed away in 1984.

He was way ahead of his time, conducting research that helped millions of migrant workers. He also wrote very interesting books, one titled *Barrio Boy*. The University of California Riverside established the Ernesto Galarza Applied Research Center.

Its website states:

> Ernesto Galarza was a man of stature. He was a man of conviction and action. He was recognized both within the Chicano community and, as witnessed by his nomination for the Nobel Peace Prize, internationally. He knew his mission in life and pursued it with a rare precision and determination. Yet Don Ernesto was also a humble man of letters.

What I have learned from my own community organizing and activism is that you do need to use academic research techniques when you research the community. You should meet with community members to make accurate assessments, and talk to senior citizens for the oral history of the place. But you should also read and analyze U.S. Census data, economic indicators, survey analysis, conduct community assessments, and continually read history books.

You also need legal advice, and even to obtain counsel in certain cases or issues. You must play many roles, including that of social worker, historian, sociologist, researcher, legal scholar, filmmaker, psychologist, psychiatrist, negotiator, talent recruitment agent, teacher, mentor, spiritual leader, fundraising expert, legal expert, and writer. By combining these roles, you can become an effective community organizer, but you must be willing to work beyond 9 to 5. You have to be available and thinking 24/7. You have to be on call, just like a medical doctor who truly cares about his or her patients. You must give your heart to the cause or social issues. Dr. Hector P. Garcia is a good example of a person of action. He helped to establish the American G.I. Forum throughout the United States. He worked tirelessly to create chapters that specifically helped Mexican American World War II veterans. Dr. Garcia took on many battles and the American G.I. Forum did help to improve the lives of many people.

As a community organizer you have to develop personal relationships and communication with key community members. You have to get to know the leaders of other non-profits and important institutions in your community. You have to be willing to attend City Council and school district meetings that may go until midnight. You have to become a good public speaker, especially if you decide to make public comments, and be willing to speak up, even if it creates animosity. Being a community organizer or activist is not a popularity contest, and you should not seek out awards or recognition. You also must pick and choose the right battles and not make unnecessary enemies. Most people will not show up and be supportive when things get hot, and many may point fingers at you for being a troublemaker. Many will make fun of activists since they may not have the courage to stand up to defend others and they rather *just talk* with no action.

You have to develop a thick skin, confidence, and good self-esteem. Many kamikazes will be sent your way to take you out. To shut you up. Even your friends may turn their backs on you or deny knowing you. Keep going, keep organizing. One day the seeds that you planted will grow and others will benefit.

You will have demands from community members and perhaps from your family too. Family members may start to see your name in the newspaper, hear you on the radio, or see you on television, advocating for social justice and community needs. Then they may believe you can help them individually. They may begin to accuse you of spending more time defending the rights of others than your own family. Yes, sometimes the sons and daughters of activists turn out great, and sometimes not so great. Sometimes because activists are so busy, their children grow up resenting them because they were not there. Sometimes grown children will accuse the father or mother of caring more for the community than for their own family.

You may find that the lines will blur between your personal and professional lives. Let's say you grew up in a low-income neighborhood, like South Central Los Angeles or Harlem and you made it out through perseverance and education, and built a career. Some family members and friends may resent you. Some may want you to provide a loan or a job. Many may think that if you attended a university and are becoming well known, then you must be making a lot of money. They do not take into account the low wages paid by many non-profits, the inadequate retirement plans, the long work hours, and the fact that you may still be struggling to pay off your student loans. Activists may feel compelled to save their own families, and play the role of hero. Of course, these are the dedicated and committed activists. You will also find the opportunistic activists who go from issue to issue, organization to organization, taking money. Legally or illegally. This is unethical and inappropriate. In your 20's you may not be able to identify these individuals, but when they have taken loans from you and never paid you back you begin to see the pattern. The "leech pattern." You will get betrayed along the way. In your 30's you may begin not to trust many people since you have been let down too many times. Many people will question your leadership and integrity, and may want to tarnish your reputation. Some will act as if they don't understand that you are working very hard to help others.

Some activists will claim that they go work for various causes and institutions because they are so effective in community organizing. Many will not admit when they are fired from campaigns or non-profits. That is why non-profits must be vigilant to do thorough background checks, legitimate reference checks, and to actually request transcripts or proof of actually graduating from a college or university. Many individuals nowadays, especially those who have questionable backgrounds and criminal records, will go to any lengths to lie on job applications and some even obtain fake reference letters and counterfeit college and university degrees.

As a seasoned activist, you may begin to understand the sacrifice and suffering of previous well known activists such as Malcolm X — who once was incarcerated and became a member of the Nation of Islam. He became a government target and his life was under constant surveillance. He did get married and had daughters that he loved very much, but he was so dedicated to Elijah Muhammad and the Nation of Islam that he was willing to give his life for it. He helped to establish various mosques throughout the United States and became an excellent organizer and public speaker. Malcolm X preached and practiced what he believed in. He was a transformed man who wanted to empower African Americans by "any means necessary." Elijah Muhammad had warned him that once he became famous, many would begin to hate him, some without even knowing him personally. He would pay the price of being an effective, committed activist.

Even some of his closest allies eventually betrayed him, and some of his own bodyguards acted out of hate, joining the plot for him to be murdered. The FBI continually tapped his phone and kept an extensive file on him. The COINTEL project was created and intended to target activists like Malcolm X, who threatened the status quo. J. Edgard Hoover, as we now know, hated individuals such as Martin Luther King and Malcolm X. He had a distinct dislike for rabble-rousers. He wanted to protect U.S. interests and status quo at all costs, even if the Constitutional rights of individuals were trampled. In death, Malcolm X became an icon and a martyr for the Black Power movement. He was embraced by many who had read the biography of him, written by Alex Haley. In this book some exaggerations were made, and the recently published book by Professor Manning Marable (now deceased), clarifies the record. This book, *A Life of Reinvention: Malcolm X,* won a 2012 Pulitzer

Prize. Professor Marable and his research assistants dug deep and obtained declassified documents that exposed some personal intimacies of Malcolm X — the man, not the activist. He had many flaws but one distinguishing characteristic was his unbreakable resilience in defending the rights of his people.

Malcolm X was ultimately betrayed and even his one-time ally Muhammad Ali (the world-famous boxer) now regrets turning his back. He was the real deal and now he is a "safe activist," since he is dead. "Finally, the convergence of interests between law enforcement, national security institutions, and the Nation of Islam undoubtedly made Malcolm X's murder easier to carry out. Both the FBI and BOSS placed informants inside the OAAU, MMI, and NOI, making all three organizations virtual rats' nests of conflicting loyalties" (Marable, 2011). Yes, Malcolm was betrayed and murdered in a cowardly manner.

Malcolm X left a legacy for other activists to learn from. They should remember that sometimes even your own community may turn its back on you. Some did stick with Malcolm X, and in the end he chose to bring different races and ethnicities together — to work towards social justice. But by then, it was too late. He had created too many powerful enemies within the Nation of Islam and the U.S. government. He was a marked man. He was also courageous and giving, and he died with no worldly possessions or money. He did not place much value on material wealth. Just imagine the horrific scene. He was murdered as his wife and daughters looked on. What a price to pay.

Each social movement had different needs and characteristics. This includes the Civil Rights movement, the United Farm Worker movement, movements for immigrant rights, environmental protection, women's rights, gay and lesbian rights, and many others, such as the movement that fights for the rights of those invisible men and women who populate our prisons.

Activists and other community leaders must pressure elected officials to help reform our criminal justice system. Today, we are warehousing 2.1 million people in jail or prison, more than any other country in the world.

Many are incarcerated because of the so-called war on drugs, which has been a huge failure and is bankrupting state budgets. "Drug offenders in prison and jails have increased 1,100 percent since 1980," according to the Sentencing Project, a nonprofit prison reform group based in Washington, D.C.

Our criminal justice system is discriminatory. "African-Americans comprise 14 percent of regular drug users, but are 37 percent of those arrested for drug offenses and 56 percent of persons in state prison for drug offenses," according to the Sentencing Project.

"More than 60 percent of the people in prison are now racial and ethnic minorities," the group notes. "For black males in their 20's, one in every eight is in prison or jail on any given day."

Many of these youth did not have opportunities to obtain a quality education, and many come from abusive households. The great majority of these youth live in poverty, and violence and incarceration are common.

Don't get me wrong. I am not defending or justifying criminal acts. Individuals who commit them need to be held responsible. But we, as a society, need to consider why violence takes place, and fairly balance the scales of our justice system.

The White House should prioritize gang prevention and intervention programs that include youth-education and job-creation elements. Such programs can counteract the hopelessness that afflicts so many of our young people of color. We must change the defeatist mentality that says, "I don't give a damn — I'm going to end up in prison anyway or I'm going to die soon."

Activists have an opportunity to continue inspiring and motivating our youth, whether they live in the urban ghettos or suburbs. To do so effectively, we need to pressure Congress and the White House to help root out the bias in our criminal justice system and support effective gang and violence-prevention programs. A generation depends on this.

Sometimes you have to live the injustices to understand what drives and motivates an activist to take on the system, the status quo, the mainstream, the government. For example, you may become an activist if your family members are beaten or murdered by the police, if your son or daughter is unjustly incarcerated, if he or she fails classes and drops out of school or gets bullied there, if you get racially profiled by the police or at the airport, or if you are mistreated or receive substandard care at the hospital.

The pain that African Americans have endured is sometimes hard for Latino activists to understand, and vice versa. Many whites have a difficult time understanding and feeling the pain that minorities endure on a daily basis, just because of their skin color or physical features. How can someone know the struggle of Latin American immigrants if they had never visited Mexico, Central America, South America, or the Caribbean except maybe as a tourist or on a cruise ship? Many of these countries are in extreme poverty, and violence is rampant. Many Latino immigrants do not come to the United States by choice — they come to avoid being tortured or murdered in their home countries. It is a dark, creepy, and disturbing history, especially in Central America where death squads were common. Many Salvadorans, for example, have horrible memories and nightmares of what occurred and continues to occur there. The violence has not ended. El Salvador is still not safe, even though more than two decades has passed since the peace accords ended the bloody civil war there.

Back in the 1980's, Central America was a political hot spot. President Reagan used inflated claims about Communism triumphing there and creeping across our southern border to justify aiding and arming death squads in El Salvador and backing the right-wing government.

The civil war against left-wing rebels claimed the lives of more than 80,000 people. Many of the murdered were innocent, working-class civilians who supported neither the soldiers nor the guerrillas. Today, the violence revolves not around politics, but around gangs. And just as the United States played a role in the civil war, so, too, does it play a role in the gang violence.

The United States is still a source of instability in El Salvador in two ways.

First, it has deported thousands of inmates who had been imprisoned for gang-related issues. The jails in El Salvador do not have the capacity to hold the never-ending numbers of inmates deported by the United States, so now many of these criminals roam the streets.

Second, the demand for illegal drugs in the United States fuels the gangs in El Salvador.

This drug trade — and the gangs that feed off it — is ruining El Salvador, since the cartels now operate extensively in Central America. One solution is for the United States to provide more aid to El Salvador to fight poverty.

A different solution, which a former GOP presidential candidate, Ron Paul, has controversially supported, is legalizing drugs in the United States to take the criminal element and the violence out of the drug trade. Sometimes you need a conservative voice to tackle such a controversial issue. Sometimes we tune out if we already know if someone is a Democrat or Republican. We have to learn to listen to each other, to see if we can work across the aisle and tackle social issues together. Senator Ted Kennedy became an expert in being able to talk and work with top Republican leaders, to help pass monumental legislation that benefited everyone. Regardless of party affiliation. Senator Kennedy was not in favor of U.S. involvement in Central America since he knew that many human rights violations were occurring, and that excessive violence was being suffered by the poor of El Salvador. Ted Kennedy had the special gift of caring for the less fortunate.

Salvadorans have not really known peace for more than 30 years now. They, like everyone else in this world, deserve a chance at a normal life. The United States should help give them that chance.

As difficult as community organizing and activism can be in the United States, it is a good deal more dangerous in many other countries. If you start questioning the government in many other countries, you run the risk of being tortured or you simply disappear. It is that serious. Many who immigrate to the United States become silent and simply obtain an education and get a safe job. Others, no longer fearing for their lives, bloom into full-time activists.

Many Central Americans were able to denounce the atrocities in their home countries once they arrived in the United States during the 1980's and early 1990's. Likewise, many South African refugees were able to also organize in the United States and other countries throughout the world, to denounce and work against apartheid.

Regardless of where activists are from, they can often face intense pressure, especially if they don't have a university degree or a big bank account. You pretty much organize because you believe in what you are fighting for. It is not for the glory or the money.

Of course, there are some activists with university degrees and millions of dollars in the bank. Some choose to be involved in causes such as environmental protection and advocacy. Many are celebrity activists like George Clooney, who do not have to worry about getting fired. Many national environmental groups are strong in resources, since some of their board members are very influential in various professional fields. You just have to analyze the Board memberships of certain environmental groups such as The Sierra Club, Audubon Society, Natural Resources Defense Council, Environmental Media Coalition, League of Conservation Voters, Tree People, and Heal the Bay. Many have well-known actors, or owners of influential corporations or consulting groups. Communities for a Better Environment (CBE) in Southeast Los Angeles does focus a lot of environmental justice work, but does not necessarily obtain the attention they deserve. CBE has been doing environmental protection work for many decades in the frontlines. Gideon Kracov, the current Board President of CBE, has been very committed and helpful in suing companies that continue to contaminate our air and water. He helped to file successful lawsuits against companies contaminating the air we breathe. Thank goodness for a few good attorneys who are willing to fight for the underdog and not necessarily for big monetary settlements. We need young leaders to become attorneys who will not become detached and arrogant.

It is imperative for activists and non-profits to build coalitions. This may sound easy, but the fact is that much infighting occurs among activists. Disputes may occur over who gets to speak at a press conference, who leads a march, who speaks at a rally, and even who is romantically involved with whom. How can we work together as activists and non-profits, when everyone is so busy organizing, mobilizing, and raising funds? It is not easy. For example, how can the Sierra Club ask to work with the labor movement when some Sierra Club members oppose immigrant rights? Some progress has been made but not enough. Just analyze the composition of the staff and Board membership of certain non-profits. Many major non-profits are not ethnically diverse at all. Also, it is important to point out that much infighting does occur among boards since many strong egos like to be heard.

Boards and corporations are not ethnically diverse, so how can they build coalitions with other groups that are, and that do grassroots organizing? This is why an activist has to know how to build personal relationships, by meeting one-on-one with key leaders and community members. You have to build trust and communication through face-to-face meetings, and you must work together on different campaigns and projects to develop a long-term relationship.

Coalition building is not easy at all. How do you bring white, black, Latino, Native American, Middle Eastern, and gay and lesbian constituencies to the same table to work together? You have to find common issues. For example, affordable health care coverage, a decent livable wage campaign, better transportation, and opposing environmental contamination are issues that can bring people together.

Finding a common cause and a passion takes a lot of work. You must transcend your own ethnicity and reach beyond the issues with which you are comfortable. If as an organizer you go into a community that is totally ethnically diverse, you will need to develop broad and lasting coalitions. You have to see how to bring together the churches, labor unions, environmental groups, immigrant rights groups, health care groups, educational rights groups, and many others, to tackle social inequities. These other community organizers must see that you are serious, and will not run when it gets tough.

You also must make a long-term commitment to long-lasting change. It is not easy. From my own experience and humble opinion, it takes an average of ten years to master issues and to develop long-lasting relationships. Coalition building is imperative for a successful activist. Sometimes the coalitions may not last long but at least you tried to build relationships. The Coalition for Humane Immigrant Rights of Los Angeles (CHIRLA) is a good example of a community group that began small, but through perseverance has become one of driving forces in immigration reform at the national level. Luke Williams and Angelica Salas have planted the seeds of a positive social movement. Angelica speaks for the voiceless and powerless. CHIRLA's spokesperson, Jorge Mario Cabrera, has been targeted by anti-immigrant and hate groups. He has evolved to become a visible and effective activist through the media. He was recently beaten up by the New York police department during a pro-immigrant rally. Luckily, activists can now take legal recourse and they can sue individuals or institutions.

One pioneering giant in the Civil Rights struggle is Morris Dees. He paved the way for many activists. According to the Southern Poverty Law Center (SPLC) web site: "he co-founded the Southern Poverty Law Center (SPLC) in 1971 following a successful business and lawcareer. He started a direct mail sales company specializing in book publishing while still a student at the University of Alabama, where he also obtained a law degree. After launching a law practice in Montgomery in 1960, he won a series of groundbreaking civil rights cases that helped integrate government and public institutions. He also served as finance director for former President Jimmy

Carter's campaign in 1976 and for Democratic presidential nominee George McGovern in 1972. Known for his innovative lawsuits that crippled some of America's most notorious white supremacist hate groups, he has received more than 20 honorary degrees and numerous awards. Those include Trial Lawyer of the Year from Trial Lawyers for Public Justice, the Martin Luther King Jr. Memorial Award from the National Education Association and The Salem Award for Human Rights and Social Justice."

Since President Obama was elected President, there has been an increase in the number of hate groups. Luckily, institutions such as the Southern Poverty Law Center still exist, and continue to be in the frontlines in fighting for civil rights and social justice. Another group that I cannot ignore is "A Better Chance (ABC)" scholarship program. ABC has improved, changed, and saved thousands of lives since 1963. They provide scholarships for inner-city students to have the option to attend great public or private high schools in other states. Lorna Holt, is a success story. She attended Foshay Junior High School from 1985 to 1988 and was accepted into A Better Chance program. She was accepted into San Dimenico School located in San Anselmo, California and she attended and graduated from Cornell University where she was a student activist within the Asociacion Latina where she served as Treasurer. She is now a top engineer at the Gas Company in Los Angeles. She has suffered and sacrificed much to continue going. She is an active member at St. Agatha's Church in Los Angeles, where she sings in the choir, and helped to establish the Stella Middle Charter School. She has a compelling personal story of persevering and serves as a positive role model for young students. Yes, we must praise and recognize the non-profit A Better Chance (ABC) program.

Chapter Ten

Other Well-Known Non-Profits and Their Role in Advocacy and Community Organizing

The National Association of Latino Elected and Appointed Officials (NA-LEO) was a brainchild of former Congressman Ed Roybal, a pioneer among Latino elected officials. NALEO was established to focus the various Latino elected officials throughout the United States on civic engagement and other types of advocacy that empower the Latino community. Arturo Vargas is its current executive director.

The Southwest Voter Registration and Education Project (SVREP) was created to focus on registering voters, and Supervisor Gloria Molina and Congressman Esteban Torres were strong advocates of SVREP. The project analyzes Latino voting, registers voters and conducts voter education projects throughout the Southwest. Its current Executive Director is Antonio Gonzalez. He is not only committed to local politics, but also international politics. He has helped to organize important delegations to other countries, especially to El Salvador and Mexico.

The National Council of La Raza (NCLR) is one of the largest and most influential Latino non-profits. It has a lot of influence in Washington, D.C., and many corporate supporters and sponsors. Janet Murguía is the current CEO.

According to NCLR's website, "As someone who has experienced the promise of the American Dream firsthand, Janet Murguía has devoted her career in public service to opening the door to that dream to millions of American families. Now, as a key figure among the next generation of leaders in the Latino community, she continues this mission as President and

CEO of the National Council of La Raza (NCLR), the largest national Hispanic civil rights and advocacy organization in the United States."

The former CEO and President of NCLR, Raul Yzaguirre, was hard-working and very influential in Washington D.C. and beyond. However, he was not immune to criticism since some felt that NCLR mainly became an elite, national, policy group, and forgot to represent the grassroots issues.

We cannot afford to ignore the League of United Latin American Citizens (LULAC), since it is one of the oldest Latino non-profits. It is very influential in Texas and has a presence in California as well, but other Latino groups are more influential and better known. In some circles, LULAC is seen as conservative, since historically it encouraged assimilation and acculturation as a means of empowerment. Many other Latino non-profits have been created in California, Texas, Arizona, Colorado, Florida, Illinois, New York and other states since the Latino population has grown tremendously in the last two decades. There are so many new Latino non-profits it would be impossible to describe all of them.

I would like to briefly mention the National Hispanic Media Coalition (NHMC), headquartered in Pasadena, CA. It advocates for hiring Latinos in the mainstream media, and denounces negative portrayals or coverage of Latinos and Latinas on television and radio and in movies and newspapers. Alex Nogales is its current executive director, CEO, and President. One example of a success story, is Jorge Nuno, who has been able to establish himself in Hollywood circles by creating images, graphics, posters, for major films. He has an activist inclination and he chose to create and establish, Nuevo South, a new non-profit organization in South Los Angeles. He runs his business and non-profit from a big classic home that he owns near the sweatshops of downtown Los Angeles. He has become involved in also advocating for USC to invest more in the surrounding poor communities. Through coalition building, Nuevo South has been successful in helping to improve South Los Angeles. But a lot more work needs to be done.

We cannot afford to ignore Mike Medavoy who is of Russian Jewish descent, but grew up in China and Chile. He is familiar with Latin America and has produced and directed remarkable worldwide films. He is now able to be very selective in which movies he makes through Phoenix Pictures. He is the Chairman and Chief Executive Officer. He knows that leadership can be lonely at the top, and that not many friends exist when we are down and out. But he has proven to be an outstanding film maker and writer, who influences millions of people through his art.

Another noteworthy organization is the Coalition for Humane and Immigrant Rights of Los Angeles (CHIRLA), one of the premier regional immigrant rights' organizations. Angelica Salas, Jorge Mario Cabrera, and the staff have dedicated their lives to defend the rights of immigrants.

Each of these nonprofits has made tremendous changes to improve the lives of countless individuals. Some of their staff members, founders, board members, and supporters have devoted their lives for their organization. Many have seen their health or their marriages suffer because they are too involved in activism, many have lost friends since they were too confrontational in their tactics and interactions, even with their allies.

Some became spiritual, others lost their faith, some turned to drugs or alcohol, while still others overcame their addictions. Some have been targeted and arrested, while many continue to play the role of choir boys and nuns, as if they could do no wrong. They may be seen as saints by some, but these activists know deep down inside that they are by no means perfect and should not be idolized. That is too much pressure for someone to live up to.

The name of Dorothy Day most likely does not ring a bell to most since she passed away in 1980. Now, New York's Cardinal Timothy M. Dolan has officially proposed for her canonization — for her to be made into a saint. The right wing, conservative Catholic movement wants to embrace her as their advocate. Ironically, she once stated "don't trivialize me by trying to make me a saint" (Otterman, 2012). In this same New York Times' article it describes her as "Dorothy Day is a hero of the Catholic left, a fiery 20th-century social activist who protested war, supported labor strikes and lived voluntarily in poverty as she cared for the need." Dorothy was an extraordinary woman. She did have an abortion as a young woman, for which Cardinal Dolan "describes her as a sinner whose life was transformed when she converted" (Otterman, 2012). She devoted her life to helping the destitute through the Catholic Church and eventually did give birth to a daughter. However, when she passed away no high-ranking Catholic bishops attended her funeral. Now the conservative wing of the Catholic Church wants to embrace her ideology by requesting that she be made into a saint. In life, she was not necessarily accepted by her own church's leadership, but now they want to capitalize on her anti-abortion position and use her legacy to push their own political agenda.

This can happen to many activists, especially in death. We see how some conservatives have tried to embrace and distort some of Martin Luther King's words to fit their own agenda. This may also happen within leftist movements. For example, El Salvador's Monsenor Romero, who was murdered by right-wing military death squads was embraced and used by the leftist guerrillas, who made him into their martyr. In fact, Monsenor Romero did not support the right or the left, since he opposed any type of violence. He was not in favor of a Civil War erupting, since he knew that much blood would be shed. He was simply on the side of the poor and the voiceless, asking the military to stop killing their own people.

Romero was gunned down by Salvadoran death squads linked to that country's military. He gave his life defending the rights of the poor and standing up to the brutality of the powerful. He was murdered on March 24, 1980. The day before he had publicly asked the Salvadoran military and National Guard to stop murdering their own brothers and sisters. After his murder came a deluge of more blood, as more than 80,000 Salvadorans were murdered, and tens of thousands tortured, during the following dozen years of civil war. Most of the deaths came at the hands of the Salvadoran military and paramilitary forces, which the U.S. government supported.

For many years, Romero served the wealthy families of El Salvador. He seemed to hide from the cruel injustices that were occurring in his country. But he had a life-changing experience when he visited a poor village known as "Los Naranjos." He realized that children were starving, and farmworkers were essentially enslaved to work the lands. He saw that they were abused and mistreated. He understood they were not allowed to speak up or to denounce injustices. If they did, then torture, beatings or death would be their fate.

Another turning point for Romero came in 1977, when his friend and fellow priest Rutilio Grande was murdered in cold blood. Following this event Romero started to speak out for the poor and the persecuted. And when the Salvadoran death squads brutally murdered labor advocates, peasant organizers, human rights workers and religious leaders, he denounced these horrors in no uncertain times.

"I would like to make a special appeal to the men of the army, and specifically to the ranks of the National Guard, the police and the military," he said in his last sermon. "Brothers, you come from our own people. You are killing your own brother peasants when any human order to kill must be subordinate to the law of God, which says, 'Thou shalt not kill.' ... I implore you, I beg you, I order you in the name of God: Stop the repression."

Thirty years have passed since Romero was murdered but his spirit and legacy are alive and well. He had to endure many accusations and defamations. He was not a communist Archbishop, as he was falsely labeled. At rock bottom, he was a true man of the cloth. Millions of Salvadorans revere Romero as a national hero. The current Archbishop of San Salvador, José Luis Escobar Alas, announced last month that he had written to Rome to ask that Romero be canonized "as soon as possible" and that the pope declare him as "San Romero de las Americas."

Archbishop Romero did not die in vain. He was, and remains, a powerful activist for his people, and the Pope should make El Salvador's Archbishop Oscar Arnulfo Romero a saint. Let's keep his legacy alive by supporting the efforts to make him a saint. He deserves no less.

Another activist that does need to be included and mentioned is Russell Means. He was a well-known Native American activist who passed away in 2012 from cancer. He became very popular in the 1970's. The New York Times described him as "...Strapping, ruggedly handsome in buckskins, with a scarred face, piercing dark eyes and raven braids that dangled to the waist, Mr. Means was, by his own account, a magnet for trouble — addicted to drugs and alcohol in his early years, and later arrested repeatedly in violent clashes with rivals and the law. He was tried for abetting a murder, shot several times, stabbed once and imprisoned for a year for rioting" (McFadden, 2012).

Mr. Means was seen by some as an opportunist, while also perceived as a hero by many. He did have a strong commitment to advocacy on behalf of Native Americans. Unfortunately, he had many other demons to fight.

The Progressive magazine interviewed Means and he stated "even though the American Indian Movement on a national-international scale has proven to be extremely dysfunctional, the American Indian Movement I was associated with I'm very proud of. We were a revolutionary, militant organization whose purpose was spirituality first, and that's how I want to be remembered. I don't want to be remembered as an activist; I want to be remembered as an American Indian patriot" (Roberts, 2012).

Activists and community leaders have many flaws that the community may not be aware of, but if they do not steal from their organization and are authentic in their activist efforts, we should not crucify them. They deserve respect, and should not be mocked or stepped on. Other activists may envy or hate a colleague's success, and disparage them or try to ruin their reputation. This is not smart politics, since no one is perfect. If you read the Bible, it states "thou shall not judge," and "Whomever is clean of any sin should throw the first stone." We are all sinners with flaws. Activists are simply individuals who seek to make a difference in the world, and care for the well-being of others. They are flawed people, nonetheless willing to speak up for the voiceless.

Chapter Eleven

How to Keep Going

Becoming an activist or community leader is a lonely road, and each journey is different. Even though conservatives tend to look down upon most activists, some of them are activists as well, who may use similar tactics, albeit while denouncing big government and holding a different world view. For example, some are National Rifle Association (NRA) activists, some protest against abortion, while others advocate for hunters. They may not like the label of activist, since it implies being a troublemaker. But regardless of the label they choose, these individuals mobilize their base and spread their message using similar activist techniques. Among other popular tools is that of religion, an organizing tool that is effective in garnering support, especially from older individuals who traditionally do attend church on Sundays.

Activists have to be responsible, and not use manipulative methods to galvanize church members for political issues that serve the interest of their particular activist or community organization. Activists must be transparent and let community members know their intentions and agenda. Trust must be built, along with the church leadership and congregation.

Many priests and pastors, especially in the Latino community, are resistant in allowing outside activists into their churches. Many thus intentionally reject any community organizing efforts, and do not particularly welcome political involvement. Some may have validity, since they may have encountered negative experiences in their home countries. One example would be a civil war, in which religious leaders were specifically targeted for their engagement in political or social causes. However, this is not an excuse for church leaders to ignore social justice issues. Former Los Angeles Cardinal Roger Mahony is a good example of a major religious leader who chose to become politically involved in openly favoring immigrant rights for decades. He personally chose to take a stand in being in favor of an immigration reform, and many times led social justice marches — literally on the streets of Los Angeles. However, revelations that he contributed in covering up Priest abuse of children, men and women have now tarnished his legacy. Catholic church members are now divided, some continue to admire Mahony's pro-immigrant and social justice work while others feel that he misled them and did not help to expose and prosecute pedophile Priests. Many times journalists and activists are the ones who expose such injustices, through spreading consciousness via newspapers and television. Activists must work to prevent such abuse.

Activists have fought for decades to make gains throughout our political process and judicial system, as well as led social movements, non-profits, media awareness campaigns, and other democratic institutions. This polarization directly threatens these accomplishments.

Sometimes a cause the activist has been working on for years or decades makes no progress at all — or sometimes things may happen too quickly. This can lead to personal temptations invading, and perhaps threatening, the work itself. Many activists along the way become addicted to substances without realizing it. Others work on campaigns, and the usual way to celebrate is to hit the bars afterward. Still others become loners, suffer depression, or abuse alcohol and/or drugs in the privacy of their own homes. Followers may not realize that their leader is addicted and needs help. Other activists do not suffer this complication. They remain clean and sober, doing excellent work throughout the decades, moving from one issue to another, having learned to keep their bodies and minds healthy. They eat well, work out, have good solid social networks, and a support system of friends and family members.

Some activists come from broken homes, single-parent homes, homes where abuse and drugs were an everyday occurrence, or they come from schools and neighborhoods full of violence. They need the adrenaline rush of activism, of protest, of denouncing injustices and taking on the oppressor, to feel alive. At home, they could not. That abusive parent or family member took their innocence and mental stability. Now the streets and protest offer an escape and a way to channel that anger, and hatred bottled up. Hatred of seeing poor people and minorities beaten and murdered by gangs, police, and seeing all sorts of disgusting and terrible things. Seeing how their neighbors were evicted since they could not afford to pay rent, seeing homeless families and abused children, witnessing domestic violence, listening to family members having sex in crowded bedrooms. Suspecting that they had a sexual predator in their own homes. Some well-known authors/activists have admitted that they were victims of abuse themselves, or had family members in their households who were sexual abusers. This is a very disturbing fact, but it does occur. It is a taboo to discuss out in the open, since much of the criticism and judgment is placed upon the victims themselves.

There are other issues that lead to anger and fury as well. Seeing how poor children could not be taken to the hospital since they have no health insurance, seeing how the public school district could care less about under-performing kids, lacking food, not being able to afford even basic necessities.

Many of these children see the increase in elected officials who are Latinos or African Americans, but they say to themselves, "Why don't they ever visit the ghetto or projects?" Perhaps it's because there is no money in the ghetto. The ghetto remains ignored, unless state or federal funds are used by developers and real estate agents to gentrify a community. This must be controlled and monitored, however. Many developers will see an opportunity to buy property and land in poor neighborhoods, and they will displace poorer residents because no one notices or cares. Let us not forget what happened at Chavez Ravine when Dodger Stadium was built. Many Mexican American homes and lots were taken away, and residents forcefully removed. Eminent domain is a perfect example how the government uses a "legal" strategy to take over private property when it is convenient. Billions of dollars are made by building freeways, shopping malls, metro rails, but many poor people never see the benefit. The kickbacks in cash are tremendous, and few elected officials get caught.

Young activists can see how corrupt our political system and society really is. They realize how favors are bought and sold. Activists have the experience of finding 100 or 200 volunteers for a political candidate, only to see the community needs forgotten once he or she gets elected. Some candidates seem to only know the activists during campaigns, when volunteers can be mobilized, contacts can be leveraged, or funds can be raised. Activists must decide whether they will continue to fight for social justice, or join the staff of an elected official, become corporate spokespeople or outreach coordinators for Wal-Mart, Coca-Cola, or other major corporations that want to give the impression of "doing the right thing." In fact, we know that many of these same corporations are contaminating our air, water, and taking away precious space and natural resources. But that activist all of a sudden will become a "company man or woman," earning over $100,000 per year, dressing in an upscale manner and driving a BMW or Mercedes Benz. Nothing is wrong with that per se, but what happened to the principles of community empowerment? Does that activist then go back and help his or her own community? Maybe. Most will justify their change of heart and lifestyle. They will say that Wall Street and corporate attorneys advised them well by telling them — "you have to think about yourself first and invest for your future." The social movement and community needs will always be there, therefore, get rich in the process. The corporate advisors will advise them to sign the contract, saying they will enable minority communities to benefit, when in fact a new freeway only contributes to more air contamination and diesel pollutants, which in turn, lead to more cancer clusters in underprivileged communities.

Let's examine Coca-Cola as a case study. The Associated Press reported in March, 2012 that "Coke directed its suppliers last year to change the way they manufacture caramel to reduce levels of the chemical 4-methylimidazole, or 4-MEI, which California has listed as a carcinogen."

This revelation offers an opportunity to delve deeper into a recent 2011 novel, "Inside Coca-Cola: A CEO's Life Story of Building the World's Most Popular Brand," by Neville Isdell with David Beasley. The book focuses on how Coca-Cola increased its market share and dominance in South Africa, the Philippines, Germany and other countries, ultimately becoming one of the most recognizable brands in the world. But what are the hidden secrets of Coca-Cola that Isdell and Beasley do not talk about? Let's examine some of them.

The book fails to mention how multinational corporations such as Coca-Cola negatively affect the availability of natural resources, especially drinking water, in developing countries, and how human rights have been violated in countries such as Colombia. It also does not admit that a caramel sweetener is a carcinogen.

Unfortunately, Coca-Cola has become part of our daily lives. Many of us have grown accustomed to having a Coke or Diet Coke with a meal — without ever thinking of its negative health effects.

Most consumers do not even realize how effective Coca-Cola marketing is. We have evolved to ignore the company's poor record on environmental issues and violations of human rights, particularly in regard to poor people in developing countries.

Isdell's job is obviously to promote Coca-Cola in a positive light, as the corporation has made him very wealthy. He does like to emphasize that he began his career at Coca-Cola as a truck driver, where he observed and learned from seasoned employees. He describes his rise in the company, ultimately to head of Coca-Cola in the Philippines. He is proud that they beat Pepsi through marketing gimmicks and political leveraging.

Isdell makes Coca-Cola seem like a righteous corporation, one that cares about developing countries and their people. He does mention how certain scandals were resolved legally, but he carefully avoids describing them in any depth.

Deval Patrick, a former Coke executive who is now governor of Massachusetts, pointed out that Coca-Cola fell short in the past when it came to promoting minorities. A lawsuit was settled out of court and the details remain confidential.

Isdell also neglects to mention how Coca-Cola has gone into certain countries to establish manufacturing plants, that in turn divert drinking water from communities to make its products. This created great controversy in

India, for example, where several activists were murdered for denouncing the diversion. In Mexico, Coca-Cola has developed a campaign titled "Super Heroes," which targets youth.

Isdell had to admit in the book that one particular lawsuit was settled accusing Coca-Cola of supporting and funding death squads in Colombia that murdered environmental activists. This is one of the reasons why Governor Patrick resigned from Coca-Cola.

Isdell also does not directly address how consuming too many soft drinks can lead to diabetes, obesity, and other health ailments. Recent research conducted by the Center for Science in the Public Interest (CSPI) indicates that the caramel coloring additives in sugar-filled beverages have contributed to cancer.

Some activists have denounced environmental groups, especially the Sierra Club, for being too cozy with certain corporations and special interest groups. For example, Isdell became so influential through Coca-Cola that he gained a board seat on the World Wildlife Fund (WWF). This ultimately benefits Coca-Cola, since they now have an ally on the inside of a worldwide environmental group. Non-profits must avoid stacking their boards with individuals who are interested in pushing the agenda of their company or corporation.

The book, although lacking in detail on controversies issues about water availability and use, provides an opportunity to question how multinational corporations harm the environments of developing countries and how human rights and labor rights are many times ignored in poor developing countries — issues that most American customers are probably not even aware of.

Some developing countries are so desperate for foreign investment that their governments will turn a blind eye when it comes to environmental, labor, and human rights abuses. Many times they are accomplices, since they also profit and become wealthy from these businesses through partnerships or outright bribery.

Coca-Cola should not be in the business of seeking profits at the expense of hurting people's health, disregarding their human rights, and degrading the environment, at home or abroad.

Remember this the next time you consider ordering "the real thing" with your next sandwich. I am not against Coca-Cola, but we must be aware that drinking too much Coca-Cola can negatively impact our health and our society.

Another example of a lifelong activist is Sister Diane Donoghue, who was part of the national campaign called "Nuns on the Bus." Her group rode throughout the United State to see how our society's inequities have created more desperation and hopelessness. But their message is of hope, and helping the most needy, no matter what. They are a great example of activists who are truly committed to helping the homeless and others who struggle with poverty.

Sister Simone Campbell, executive director of NETWORK, was interviewed recently about what it is like to help the broken. Yes, these older ladies bring hope, and lead by example. They are the Good Samaritans in our society. I can see the kindness in their personalities and work. They remind me of the nuns that were murdered in El Salvador. They were doing God's work, but were accused of being Communist agitators. What a sad statement on our society when closed-minded individuals label activists as Socialist or Communist. That is such an old strategy of hate and division. We know that McCarthyism destroyed many lives in the United States, by accusing activists of being communist. Many of them were simply advocating for social justice and equality for all.

The poor and the homeless should not be punished for simply asking for help. We need to do more now than ever, to address the problem of homelessness. Homeless rates are rising in the United States at record levels, due to our severe economic crisis.

In 2009, President Obama was asked about the problem at a press conference. To his credit, he gave a compassionate response, "Part of the change in attitudes that I want to see here in Washington and all across the country," the president said, "is a belief that it is not acceptable for children and families to be without a roof over their heads in a country as wealthy as ours."

Despite that talk, several years later families make up 34 percent of the homeless population, and one in every 50 children is homeless in America, according to the National Center on Family Homelessness.

The homeless are disproportionately black and brown, 43 percent black and 15 percent Hispanic, according to the center. And the faces of the homeless are getting younger, especially among the Latino community.

Many Latino parents who end up homeless do not speak English, and some do not know where to seek aid. Sadly, some organizations that work on homeless issues do not know how to reach out to them.

For children, homelessness is especially tragic. They worry about where they're going to sleep at night. They worry about their own safety, and that of their parents. They often feel ashamed and keep it a secret from their teachers or school administrators. Many have difficulty concentrating on schoolwork and cannot do their homework under a bridge, or in a cramped, smelly, cheap motel rooms where illicit activities are rampant. They move from one school district to another, making it even harder for them to get good grades.

As taxpayers, all of us, we must demand that our government work towards alleviating this problem. Instead of just bailing out and saving countless financial, automobile, mortgage, and insurance institutions, our government should also help the homeless children in our midst. Investing in these children would cost a mere fraction of the cost of bailing out corporate America. And we have a moral imperative to do this.

Insufficient funding for homeless children must not be tolerated any longer. Let's not ignore the homeless issue. Let's not pretend that homeless children do not exist. They do, and we aren't doing enough to help them. In Pasadena, a few local activists are unsung heroes in this arena. They include, Socorro Rocha, who heads up Pasadena Unified School District's Families in Transition program. She helps countless homeless families and children through food, shelter, and clothing. Socorro is a tireless advocate and she who means what she says. Another advocate, Robin Salzer, owns Robin's BBQ Restaurant in Pasadena, and decided to take matters into his own hands. He began providing free hot meals for the homeless, using his own resources. He is a Republican and his wife, Anne-Marie Villalcana, was the first Latina elected to the Pasadena City Council. Marge and Joe Wyatt are two other iconic leaders in Pasadena. Marge was elected to the Pasadena School Board in 1977 and served until 1985. She was Board President from 1979 to 1985, and was a staunched supporter of former Pasadena Unified School District Superintendent Ray Cortines. They were both in the middle of the battles to desegregate Pasadena public schools. Ray was fired by the conservative PUSD school board majority, but was so popular that he was asked to return by former school board member Elbie Hickambottom. Elbie was a retired Army Major, first elected to the PUSD school board in 1979, where he served for 16 years. Elbie's wife, Dolores Hickambottom, continues to be an active community leader in the San Gabriel Valley.

Another advocate, Renatta Cooper, has actively and effectively served as the President of the Pasadena Unified School District Board of Education (PUSD). She had to take on many battles, especially with a few of her school board member colleagues who have different points of views and political interests.

Renatta, as she is warmly known in Pasadena, has made it a priority to stand up for the rights of youth. According to the Pasadena Unified School District official web-site it states:

> Prior to her election to the Board of Education, Ms. Cooper taught graduate-level child development courses at Pacific Oaks College in Pasadena, where she helped create and fund the Hixon Center for Early Childhood.

Renatta also served as a member of the "First 5" L.A. Commission, the group that was formed with the passage of a state initiative, headed by Rob Reiner, to fund the development of early childhood education centers in Los Angeles County, from 2001-05. She took a leadership role in the development and passage of the $500 million Universal Preschool Initiative, the $32 million

Family Literacy Initiative, and the $27 million Workforce Development Initiative.

Since 2005, she has worked as an educational coordinator in the Los Angeles County Chief Administrator's Office. Renatta is the liaison between the County Office of Child Care and other organizations concerned with strengthening the early childhood workforce to improve the educational outcomes of young children in Los Angeles County.

Renatta graduated cum laude with a degree in Early Childhood Education from Towson State University in Baltimore, and earned a masters in Human Development, with a specialization in multicultural studies, from Pacific Oaks College in Pasadena. Born in Berkeley, California, Renatta is a resident of Pasadena, and a proud Pasadena High School Bulldog."

Renatta Cooper continues to dedicate much time and effort to help improve public education. Being a school board member is challenging, due to the fact that public education issues are highly political and controversial. We must do a better job of acknowledging and applauding elected officials who truly care about given back to the community and who consciously choose not to *sell out* to certain special interests or small yet influential interest groups that wield too much economic power. Sometimes these special interest groups feel that they can literally buy politicians. Politicians must be reminded that it is the voters who decide whether they remain in office or not. Therefore, voting can be quite powerful in making positive social change that ultimately benefits everyone. Another former elected official that is noteworthy to highlight is Trent Fluegel. He served as a house director, along with his wife Becky, for the Rochester Better Chance (RBC) program. They were my house parents while I attended high school in Rochester, Minnesota. Trent decided to run to represent the needs of recent immigrant students. He stood up for the rights of students who emigrated to Rochester, MN from Southeast Asia and Somalia. He was an activist school board member who was eventually defeated but he brought issues that others did not dare to bring up. He also served as the executive director for Habitat for Humanity in Rochester. He has helped countless people through his humanity. Trent and his wife Becky were also the house directors at the Rochester Better Chance (RBC) program — while my housemates and I attended John Marshall High School in Rochester, Minnesota.

Chapter Twelve

All You Need Is Love — and Ganas

What a beautiful song, *All You Need Is Love,* and yes, love brings joy and hope. Hopefully activist and community leaders and non-profits will not just bring love, but also opportunities and programs to improve our everyday lives. Much responsibility falls on MALDEF, MAOF, El Centro de Accion Social, and many other non-profits in our society. Non-profits are expected to do miracles with limited budgets. Now government help and grants are being cut. Non-profits are relying more on foundations, corporations, and individual donors to survive. It is a tough job to be an Executive Director. You therefore need to have *ganas.* That is what Professor Escalante used to tell his students at Garfield High School. He wanted them to believe in themselves, to learn calculus, and to become professionals. Very few Executive Directors in the last few years are running the same non-profit organizations, since the pressures are usually tremendous. Ganas — motivation — perseverance — are key ingredients to keep going.

As the safety valve for our most needy, non-profits also create millions of jobs and contribute billions of dollars to our economy. Sometimes non-profits and private foundations provide creative solutions to social challenges.

The life of helping others can be crazy and difficult. But activists should choose to "stay in the kitchen even when it gets hot." They should be leading marches, protests, and press conferences, helping to build homes, giving away food and clothing, creating scholarships, raising money, being public speakers, being motivational role models, choosing civil disobedience to send a social message, charting a course for others to follow, and creating opportunities for others to benefit. Being an activist is not a license for being selfish or self-centered. You have to be a giving person, a person with a kind heart and the courage to fight for social justice. But you also have to set a limit so that you will not be used for someone else's benefit or hidden agenda. That is a particularly tricky part. But if you are acting from the heart — that is all that matters. You are acting for reals even when others are profiting from you.

This is my second book, and I hope it helps to serve both young and seasoned activists. An activist's career is filled with mine fields, but can be extremely rewarding. Imagine saying that you marched for Civil Rights! That you marched with Cesar Chavez to defend the rights of the migrant workers. That you walked with Gandhi to liberate the Indian people from British domination. That you supported Nelson Mandela to end Apartheid in South Africa. That you helped to denounce the atrocities occurring in Central America. That you risked your life by denouncing environmental injustices. That you helped to build homes with Jimmy Carter's Habitat for Humanity. That you helped to elect a candidate who promoted incredible legislation that benefited thousands of people. That you chose to get arrested to defend the rights of your community. In the process, some activists may become immersed in debt and file for bankruptcy. For others marriages will be broken, divorce may occur, child custody battles will occur, but you have to keep going. That is the price you have to pay along the way. You must continue to sacrifice for others' well-being.

Activism is like planting seeds that take years to sprout. Activism is an everyday job. You have to avoid becoming an oppressor and focusing on monetary rewards or recognition. Of course, there is nothing wrong with obtaining recognition but it has to be done in an authentic manner — one must not do things just to seek the limelight. Pretty soon community members are able to see who is in it for real.

Activism is about helping others, not necessarily becoming rich. It's ok if you make a good salary. Especially if you know that you walked the neighborhoods, met with community members, helped stuff envelopes, made phone calls, and sweated to earn that well-earned pay check. It is rewarding to get a college education, and then choose to become an activist. You are using your knowledge to help others. We have to learn to forgive those who betrayed us. We have to learn not to judge an activist who is truly trying to help, but may not know how to do it. That activist will learn from his or her mistakes. Let's help the up- and-coming activist who wants to make social change. Let us also help that activist who may idealize, romanticize the needs of the poor, and may take a paternalistic approach in trying to help disenfranchised community members. Let us give advice to that old timer activist who thinks that he or she has to pretend to know barrio or ghetto lingo, by using thug like language. For example, would they address a key funder as homeboy or homegirl? Would they act as if they are too important or busy to meet with a fellow activist? Yes. And we must not waste our time with activists who have become arrogant, and pretend to be all knowing. Let us professionally counsel the activist who uses bad words when referring to other activists or community members. Sometimes we need to get fired, when merited, to learn life lessons.

Recently, I attended an environmental fundraiser, and I bumped into many old friends and colleagues. One activist in particular, was constantly using foul and offensive language, which came across as highly unprofessional and completely unnecessary. I asked him if he had been drinking and he said "no," and began to share his "tough guy" stories about how he had beat up people. We have to teach these types of activists that violence or bad words are not necessary to make a point, or to make social change. Being an effective and authentic activist carries much responsibility, and power should not be misused. Why replicate the attitude and actions of corrupt individuals? It is not necessary.

Put on that activist hat and uniform. You can feel like Batman, Spiderman, or Superman, when you help to win issues that benefit the people. You may become a hero for those young kids who have never met a real-life hero. You will become a better person when you meet others who are suffering and you see that they begin to rely on you.

But do not get lost in that process. Be conscious and aware that you need to take care of your physical and mental well- being. Do not allow yourself to become a victim. You will make mistakes, but learn from them. Try to avoid repeating them, and teach others the lessons you've learned. Share the experience of working in terrible, abusive jobs where your boss and others stepped on you, but you persevered. Share stories of classmates who made fun of you, but you did not listen and kept going. Share experiences of that time you got arrested for driving under the influence and learned not to do that again. You may risk being labeled a drunkard, but who the hell cares, since people will always judge those who make mistakes. But do they look at their own weaknesses and faults? Maybe your mistakes will make them look in the mirror and admit their own shortcomings. Others may get inspiration to keep going, once they learn that you have failed at certain things, too. No one is perfect.

Share that story of when you got arrested for protesting in favor of immigrant rights. Share that story of when your friends were shot and killed. Share that story of your friends ending up with a long prison term or a life sentence. Share your stories of pain and triumphs. That young person may be listening to you when you share your stories and may choose the right path. You never know, maybe others will choose to become activists and community leaders — por vida.

Chapter Thirteen

The Purpose of Being an Activist —
Is This Love?

The point of this book is not to come across as an angry activist, but to create social change. If you are complacent and accommodating, then change will most likely not occur. You can be both angry and pragmatic. The life of an activist is turbulent and difficult, and also extremely rewarding. You can learn many valuable lessons by being in the trenches of social justice movements. We must give credit to activists from the past — those who gave their lives to the Civil Rights movement, immigrant rights, gay and lesbian rights, and those who continue the legacy well into their mature age. We must not forget who they were, and what they contributed to improving society for all. We have to learn from the old-timers who gave their very heart and soul for social justice.

Overall, the point is not to lose yourself in self-destructive activities. The goal is to grow and blossom as an activist, and as a community organizer. To mature as a human being so you can see society's inequities, and develop and share the knowledge and experience to change them. As Gandhi stated, "Be the change you want to see in the world." Change comes first within our mind, heart, and soul. Once you gain knowledge, spiritual strength, and a vision of empathy, then you can begin to change the community around you. First, be at peace with yourself. Then if you choose to risk your life and stability will be a conscious decision. Know that the price of activism may be costly. However, we must seek social change through non-violence. And to do that, we must practice non-violence in our everyday lives. We must restrain ourselves from physically hurting others, taking revenge, or plotting to hurt someone.

Ideally we must be activists who can take life lessons and the best examples of other leading well-known activists that we admire, and put them into use. Imagine having the perseverance and patience of Nelson Mandela? The limitless love of Mother Theresa? The courage of the Dalai Lama? Start with being yourself. Accept your own strengths and weaknesses. An activist who knows him or herself, who is spiritually in touch, can be a very powerful individual.

If you choose the crazy life of an activist, it is my hope that this book will provide the necessary tools for your journey. You will stumble and make mistakes, but do not give up. An activist must have endurance and knowledge. Begin by reading other books about social movements, politics, economics, history, sociology, activism, and leadership. Then get out there. Only by doing the everyday work of social change and communicating with others, will you ultimately become a leader and an activist. Along the way, stay calm and focused. Always believe in yourself, and your own God-given abilities, talents, and gifts.

How to start? Might as well organize a march or a peace walk in your community. Why not? It is never too late to make a difference in the world. Might as well lead by example, through love, forgiveness, generosity, and kindness. Let us remember, we are all in this together.

I want to finish with Bob Marley's lyrics from *Is This Love* playing in the background. Yes, let's give some love to activists everywhere in the world. Don't stop believing in yourself and never give up.

Appendix

Excerpt of interview conducted by Corina Martinez Chaudhry, *CEO of* www.TheLatinoAuthor.com

Tell us a little bit about yourself; where you grew up, city where you currently reside, family upbringing, or anything you would like our readers to know about you?

I was born in Los Angeles. However, at eight months old, my mother and I were deported to El Salvador. I grew up there till age 5, then returned and grew up in South Central Los Angeles. I currently live in the San Gabriel Valley.

I have had both rural and urban experiences. I have survived both thick and thin of things, trials and tribulations. That is why I write, to motivate and inspire others to succeed in life. To not be ashamed of mistakes made, cause everyone sins, whether through deeds, or in our minds when we say or think ill things of others.

Your first book Hope in Times of Darkness: A Salvadoran American Experience *discusses your experiences of growing up Salvadoran in both in El Salvador and the U.S. What was the big reason you decided to write about this and what did you hope to accomplish?*

I have read many, many books in my life, and I am still enamored with the written word. I loved certain books as a child from John Steinbeck and others. I discovered Latino literature at Occidental College, and began to read works by James Baldwin, Alex Haley, Oscar Zeta Acosta, Carlos Fuentes, Gabriel Garcia Marquez, and Maxine Hong Kingston. I read Maya Angelou and *The Diary of Anne Frank* in middle school. I think that I read the whole section related to Latin America (especially El Salvador related) at the Occidental College library.

Eventually, I wanted to write my own story from my own perspective, in a non-fiction, narrative manner. I wanted to share my point of view on some of the injustices and inequities that I have lived through and witnessed firsthand. I saw violence, murders, chaos, and I wanted to express myself through the written word.

Writing a memoir can be a healing experience. Did you find this to be true?

It is not necessarily a memoir since I am not too old. It is more a non-fiction, narrative; to tell the story of the sacrifice and suffering of the Latino and African American community in South Central Los Angeles. How many Latino authors have come from South Central? Not many. My book is a universal story that any race, ethnicity, or nationality can relate to.

Yes, it can be a healing, yet not so healing process, since writing brings up so many memories as well as anger. But eventually it creates hope. That is what I try to do — turn anger, frustration, and bitterness into a more positive perspective. We grow through sacrifice, pain, and suffering. I can relate to young people who have to live in violent neighborhoods and schools.

Once you decided to write your first book, how long did it take you to complete?

I wrote it in one summer. I was really motivated and inspired. But it took me about one year with the editing process, and another year to be accepted by two publishers.

Did you always want to write or did this desire to do so come later in life?

I did not necessarily realize that I had the power to write a book. One day something clicked. I had just read Victor Villasenor and was also inspired by Luis Rodriguez' writing, perseverance, and example. It's similar to how I did not know that I could bench press 400 lbs. Writing is similar to power lifting — you have to lift one pound at a time, and you have write one word at a time.

Was it the technique of writing, publishing it, or marketing it thereafter?

There is no one technique. It is a road with many roadblocks and naysayers. You have to keep writing from your heart, from your life experiences, and you have to do it almost every day to become proficient at it. Of course, you never really become a master or perfect at it. We always make mistakes as humans. For example, the classic books all have mistakes. Therefore, it is true — no one is perfect. If you can find a perfect person I would like to write their biography.

What steps would you suggest a writer take before they begin on writing a memoir?

Practice, practice, and practice. Be ready to expose yourself to the world, the good and the bad. You will be judged. Get ready for a roller coaster ride whether you like it or not.

You were born here, your mother was then deported, but she chose to take you back with her rather than leave you here alone. Can you talk about that experience and how that shaped your life?

I believe that can be traumatic for any child, especially when you are a baby. Then my grandparents helped raise me in the countryside because my mother had to work in San Salvador. Pain is being torn from your parents. Pain is when your child is taken away from you. When I returned to Los Angeles at the age of five and didn't know English, it was a nightmare! I suffered a lot.

Eventually, I learned English and began to accept and learn the traditions and cultures of the U.S. I learned the language by watching Scooby Doo, The Land of the Lost, The Streets of San Francisco, and The Justice League. I still remember "MASH," the "LAVERNE & SHIRLEY" and THREE'S COMPANY theme songs. My favorite show was the "TWILIGHT ZONE." That show had some powerful political messages.

Who or what inspires you?

God, first, and then all of the special people in my life. They have struggled and suffered much but we are still here, working and trying to make a difference for our sons, daughters, nephews, nieces, cousins...trying to set a good example. Even if we screw up, we can still get up and keep going.

I also get inspiration from people who have been down and out, who have had drug and alcohol addictions and chose to turn their lives around for the better. It is possible — not easy, but possible. I get inspiration from music too: Shakira, Tupac, Notorious B.I.G., Nortenas, Selena, classical music, jazz, and the teachings of Gandhi. I sometimes listen to heavy metal and classic rock, too — it depends on the mood.

If you had to define success, how would you define it?

Having love in your heart and being able to forgive. To try very hard not to judge others. Have we walked in their shoes to know their pain?

Their addictions? Their anger?

Many times we have to travel that tough road to know how hard it is to make it out of the ghetto and violent/abusive situations. Sometimes people feel trapped, but through writing, we can inspire others not to feel trapped.

That is why I chose to write my second book. *The Life of an Activist: In the Frontlines 24/7.*

References

Beasley, D. Isdell, N. (2011). *INSIDE Coca-Cola.* New York: St. Martin's Press.

Bobb, J.M. (2012). *The Los Angeles County Sheriff's Department 31 st Semiannual Report.* Police Assessment Resource Center (PARC).

Carter, S. (1999). *Civility.* New York: Harper Perennial. ISBN: 0060977590.

City of Pasadena (2012). *Pasadena/Altadena Quality of Life Index.* City of Pasadena Public Health Department.

Cook, C.D. (2012, November). The Progressive Interview: Robert Reich. *The Progressive,* 76, Number 11, 35-38.

Druckner, P. F. (1990). *Druckner: Managing the Non-Profit Organization,* London: Part of Reed International Books.

Gottlieb, H. (2008). Board Recruitment and Orientation, Tucson: Renaissance Press.

Hall, M. (2009). Union Membership Grows in 2008. When People Can Join Unions, They Do. *AFL-CIO Now Blog News.* Retrieved from http://blog.aflcio.org/2009/01/28/union-membership-grows-in-2008-when-people-can-join-unions-they-do/.

Harvard Business Essentials (2002). *Finance for Managers.* Boston: Harvard Business School Press.

Harvard Business Review (2011). *Blockbuster's Former CEO on Sparring with an Activist Shareholder.* Boston: Harvard Business Publishing.

Ingram R.T. (2009). Ten Basic Responsibilities of Nonprofit Boards, Second Edition. *Board-Source.* Retrieved June 16, 2012, from http://www.urban.org/nonprofits/highimpactphilanthropy.cfm.

Marable, M. (2011). *A Life of Reinvention: Malcolm X.* New York: Viking Press.

McFadden, R.D. (2012, October 22). Russell Means, Who Revived Warrior Image of American Indian, Dies at 72. *The New York Times.* Retrieved from http://www.nytimes.com/2012/10/23/us/russell-means-american-indian-activist-dies-at-72.html?pagewanted=1&_r=0&hp.

Meyer, R. E. (2012, October 21). George McGovern, liberal standard-bearer against Nixon in '72, dies. *L.A. Times.* Retrieved from http://www.latimes.com/news/la-me-george-mcgovern-20121021,0,7105562,full.story.

Orwell, G. (2003). *Animal Farm,* New York: Plume/Harcourt Brace Book.

Otterman, S. (2012, November). In Hero of the Catholic Left, a Conservative Cardinal Sees a Saint. *The New York Times.* Retrieved from http://www.nytimes.com/2012/11/27/nyregion/sainthood-for-dorothy-day-has-unexpected-champion-in-cardinal-timothy-dolan.html?pagewanted=all&pagewanted=print&_r=0.

Roberts, C. (2012, October). *Russell Means, in Memoriam.* The Progressive. Retrieved from http://www.progressive.org/russell-means-in-memoriam.

Rolling Stone (2012, December 27). John Lennon: The Ultimate Guide to His Life, Music & Legend.

Shakely, J. (2012, April 30). The worst way to judge a charity. *Los Angeles Times*. Retrieved from http://www.latimes.com/news/opinion/commentary/la-oe-shakely-charity-rating-kahneman-20120430,0,5220795.story.

The Andrew J. Mellon Foundation web site (2012, April 30). Retrieved from http://www.mellon.org/about_foundation/mission.

The Mexican American Legal Defense and Educational Fund web site (2012, June 16). Retrieved from http://www.maldef.org/about/mission/index.html.

The Mexican American Opportunity Foundation web site (2012, June 16). Retrieved from http://www.maof.org/.

The Urban Institute web site (2013, January 16). Retrieved from http://www.urban.org/nonprofits/highimpactphilanthropy.cfm.

Wilcox, P.J. (2006). *Exposing the elephants: Creating Exceptional Nonprofits*, New Jersey: John Wiley & Sons, Inc.

Willon, P. (2009, July 15). L.A. mayor's chief counsel tapped to lead MALDEF. *Los Angeles Times*. Retrieved from http://articles.latimes.com/2009/jul/15/local/me-saenz15.

Index